Written by   Nancy Shaw
Edited by   Linda Milliken
Design by   Wendy Loreen
Illustrated by   Barb Lorseyedi
Cover Illustration by   Priscilla Burris

© 1993 **Edupress** • P.O. Box 883 • Dana Point, CA 92629

ISBN 1-56472-023-3

Table of Contents

LITERATURE SELECTIONS

Format:

❊ The literature selections are presented in two categories—fiction and non-fiction.

❊ Suggested reading levels are located in parentheses and are arranged in grade-level order beginning with grade 2. These are publishers' suggested reading levels and may vary according to student ability.

❊ Up-to-date publication information has been referenced. However, books are continually going "out of print" and you may be unable to locate a specific title. Refer to *Best Books for Children,* (R.R. Bowker), a subject guide for children's literature, for additional titles or substitutions. This book is available in the reference center of your local library.

Uses:

❊ Reproduce and send home a copy of the literature selections for parents to use when assisting their children with reading choices.

❊ Refer to suggested titles when planning whole-language curriculum. You may choose to use books as "read-aloud" resources.

❊ Refer to book summaries to help children select books of interest to them.

❊ Encourage children to read several books within the same theme in order to develop their understanding of plot development, setting, and character differences within a similar theme.

RELATED STUDIES

❊ Look here for assistance when planning thematic curriculum.

❊ Encourage children to explore topics "on their own" by using the list of related studies as additional reading prompts.

ACTIVITY

❊ Extend learning cooperatively or individually with multicurricular activity suggestions.

BOOK REPORT FORMS

❊ Reproduce for individual use. As a general rule, content is geared for both fiction and non-fiction titles. Be sure to discuss the difference with children.

❊ Use the generic form as a springboard for cooperative group discussion. Encourage discussion of similarities and differences of books with the same general theme.

© EDUPRESS

• Fiction •

LITERATURE SELECTIONS

❀ *Patti's Pet Gorilla*
by Pat Rhoads Mauser; Macmillan 1987. (2-4)
Patti wants to impress her classmates at show-and-tell, so she tells them she has a pet gorilla.

❀ *The Day Jimmy's Boa Ate the Wash*
by Trinka Hakes Noble; Dial 1980. (2)
A wild class trip to a farm sets off a chain of silly disasters when a student brings his boa constrictor.

❀ *Henry and Mudge*
by Cynthis Rylant; Macmillan 1987. (2-3)
The story of how Henry, a boy, and Mudge, a very large dog, get together.

❀ *Esmeralda and the Pet Parade*
by Cecile Schoberle; Simon & Schuster 1990. (2-3)
The story of young Juan and the antics of his mischievous pet goat.

❀ *Wally*
by Judie Wolkoff; Bradbury 1977. (3-4)
Michael agrees to reptile-sit his friend's pet snake for two weeks—against his mother's instructions.

❀ *Fudge*
by Charlotte Graeber; Lothrop 1987. (3-5)
Chad's parents say he can have a puppy, but no one has time to train it.

❀ *Gentle Ben*
by Walt Morey; Dutton 1965. (4-5)
Mark struggles to keep his beloved Alaskan brown bear, in the northern Alaskan town of Orca City.

❀ *Harry's Mad*
by Dick King-Smith; Crown 1987. (4-5)
Harry inherits a talking parrot named Madison who can play the piano and use the telephone.

• Non-Fiction •

LITERATURE SELECTIONS

❀ *Taking My Cat to the Vet*
by Susan Kuklin; Bradbury 1988. (2-3)
Color photos highlight this first-person story of what happens when a cat goes to the veterinarian.

❀ *Pets*
by Illa Podendorf; Childrens LB 1981. (2-3)
A very simple account that features many color photographs.

❀ *Cats*
by Elsa Posell; Childrens 1983. (2-4)
Some wild cats are introduced, but the concentration is on the cat as a pet.

❀ *Bonny's Big Day*
by James Herriot; St. Martin's 1987. (3-4)
A Yorkshire farmer is persuaded by a veterinarian to enter his old cart-horse into a show.

❀ *Owls in the Family*
by Farley Mowat; Little, Brown 1962. (3-5)
The author describes two wild horned owls, Wols and Weeps that he found and tamed when he was a boy

❀ *Pets Without Homes*
by Caroline Arnold; Houghton 1983. (2-5)
Through the story of a lost puppy, a city's animal control department is studied.

❀ *My Parrot Eats Baked Beans: Kids Talk about Their Pets*
by Barbara Garland Polikoff; Whitman 1988. (3-5)
Interviews and photos of children and their pets.

❀ *A Service Dog Goes to School: The Story of a Dog Trained to Help the Disabled*
by Elizabeth Simpson Smith; Morrow LB 1988. (3-5)
The story of Licorice from a puppy to canine school.

RELATED STUDIES & ACTIVITY

● Veterinarians ● House Pets ● Pet Care ● Pet Training ● Snakes ●

● Have a pet-sharing day. Invite students to bring pictures and share stories about their pets. ●

PETS

Title _____   **Author** _____

Describe the pet in the story.

Tell what is unusual, funny, different or special about the pet in the book.

What did the pet owner do to care for their pet?

Would you want to be the pet in the story? Tell why or why not.

DINOSAURS

● Fiction ●

LITERATURE SELECTIONS

❂ **The First Dog**
by Jan Brett; Harcourt 1988. (2)
After a hungry Paleowolf warns Kip of danger, Kip
brings the creature home and names him "Dog."

❂ **We're Back!**
by Hudson Talbott; Crown 1987. (2-3)
Seven dinosaurs voyage to New York's Museum of
Natural History, in time for Macy's annual parade.

❂ **Danny and the Dinosaur**
by Syd Hoff; HarperCollins 1958. (2-3)
A museum dinosaur spends a perfectly wonderful
day wandering around the city with Danny.

❂ **Big Old Bones: A Dinosaur Tale**
by Carol Carrick; Ticknor 1989. (2-3)
The author explains how all evidence for dinosaurs is
deduced from fossils.

❂ **Dinosaurs are 568**
by Jean Rogers; Greenwillow 1988. (2-4)
Raymond consents to attend school only when he is
told he can learn about dinosaurs.

❂ **T. Rex's Missing Tooth**
by Jacqueline Ball; HarperCollins 1991. (4-5)
A Tyrannosaurus has a problem with a missing tooth
and chaos ensues.

❂ **Sneeze-O-Saurus**
by Jacqueline Ball; HarperCollins 1990. (4-5)
Imagine what might happen if a thunderous
Stegosaurus just happened to sneeze?

❂ **The Enormous Egg**
by Oliver Butterworth; Little, Brown 1956. (4-5)
An ordinary chicken hatches a dinosaur egg, giving
Nate his own pet triceratops.

● Non-Fiction ●

LITERATURE SELECTIONS

❂ **Supersaurus**
by Francine Jacobs; Putnam LB 1982. (2-3)
The story of the discovery of bones from a giant
dinosaur.

❂ **Be a Dinosaur Detective**
by Dougal Dixon; Lerner 1988. (2-4)
The author explains how all evidence for dinosaurs is
deduced from fossils.

❂ **Dinosaurs**
by Daniel Cohen; Doubleday LB 1987. (2-4)
A look at the dinosaurs when they inhabited the
earth.

❂ **Dinosaurs Are Different**
by Aliki; HarperCollins 1985. (2-4)
The differences among the giant creatures are
explained in simple text and clear pictures.

❂ **Digging Up Dinosaurs**
by Aliki; HarperCollins 1981. (2-4)
This book provides a look at how dinosaurs got from
the ground into museums.

❂ **The News About Dinosaurs**
by Patricia Lauber; Bradbury 1989. (3-5)
What scientists used to believe about dinosaurs
versus what they now feel is true.

❂ **Dinosaurs**
by Lee Bennett Hopkins; Harcourt 1987. (3-5)
A universally adored reptile such as this deserves its
own collection, including the full-paged drawings.

❂ **The Monsters Who Died: A Mystery about**
  Dinosaurs
by Vicki Cobb; Putnam 1983. (3-5)
An exploration of how we found out about dinosaurs.

RELATED STUDIES & ACTIVITY

● Prehistoric Era ● Fossils ● Lizards ● Meat and Plant Eaters ●
● Using the medium of choice, make a model of a dinosaur ●

DINOSAURS

Title

_____

Author

_____

If you could ask the dinosaur in the book two questions, what would they be?

_____

_____

What did you learn about dinosaurs that you didn't know before?_____

_____

_____

What problems did (or would) having a pet dinosaur create?   _____

_____

_____

Draw a picture of something the dinosaur in the book might eat.

List three things bigger than the dinosaur in the book.

LITERATURE SELECTIONS

❋ *Worm Day*
by Harriet Ziefert; Viking 1987. (2-3)
Mr. Rose's class heads out to collect samples and learn about worms.

❋ *Much Ado About Aldo*
by Johanna Hurwitz; Morrow 1978. (2-3)
When the class crickets face being eaten by the class chameleons, Aldo becomes a vegetarian.

❋ *Fourth Grade Rats*
by Jerry Spendle; Scholastic 1991. (2-3)
Alroy's fear of spiders will never get him into a coveted club.

❋ *Two Bad Ants*
by Chris Van Allsburg; Houghton Mifflin 1988. (3-4)
Two ants journey to gather crystals for the ant queen and decide to stay.

❋ *Beetles, Lightly Toasted*
by Phyllis Naylor; Macmillan 1987. (4-5)
Andy must test his essay premise that beetles are good eating.

❋ *Charlottes's Web*
by E.B. White; HarperCollins 1952. (3-4)
Wilbur, a pig, is saved from slaughter by Charlotte, the gray spider in the barnyard door.

❋ *Shoebag*
by Mary James; Scholastic 1990. (4-5)
A contented young cockroach awakens one morning to find he has been transformed into a little boy.

❋ *The Winter Worm Business*
by Patricia Reilly Giff; Delacorte 1981. (4-5)
Leroy digs worms to sell for fishing bait with his good friend Tracy.

LITERATURE SELECTIONS

❋ *A First Look at Caterpillars*
by Millicent Selsam; Walker LB 1988. (2-3)
Discusses caterpillar parts and the process of metamorphosis.

❋ *Bugs*
by Nancy W. Parker/Joan Richards Wright; Greenwillow LB 1987. (2-3)
Provides solid—and fascinating—facts about 16 common bugs.

❋ *Ant Cities*
by Arthur Dorros; Crowell 1987. (2-3)
Explains how ants build their nests and run their empires with the queen in charge.

❋ *Earthworms*
by Chris Henwood; Watts 1988. (3-4)
Lively photos help to describe these slithery creatures.

❋ *Where Do They Go? Insects in Winter*
by Millicent E. Selsam; Macmillan 1982. (3-4)
How twelve species of insects cope with the harsh weather of winter.

❋ *Discovering Slugs and Snails*
by Jennifer Coldrey; Watts 1987. (4-5)
The story of Thomas Small and the threat to the treasure of Drear House.

❋ *Discovering Spiders*
by Malcolm Penny; Watts 1986. (4-5)
Find out how spiders live and spin their webs.

❋ *Nature's Living Lights: Fireflies And Other Bioluminescent Creatures*
by Alvin Silverstein; Little 1988. (4-5)
Explores the creatures and insects that seem to glow.

RELATED STUDIES & ACTIVITY

● Insects ● Spiders ● Butterflies ● Moths ● Caterpillars ● Metamorphosis ● Webs ●

● Go on a walk to look for insects and other crawling creatures. Make an observation log. ●

CREEPY CRAWLY CREATURES

Title

Author

Imagine you are the creepy, crawly creature you read about and write your "autobiography."

It all started when

Let me describe myself.

My home is

My biggest fear is

My most memorable moment was when

● Fiction ●

LITERATURE SELECTIONS

❋ ***The Ugly Duckling***
by Hans Christian Andersen; Harcourt 1979. (2)
A classic story about a swan's miserable childhood.

❋ ***Song of the Swallows***
by Leo Politi; Macmillan 1987. (2-3)
Juan rings the mission's bells to welcome the
swallows returning to San Juan Capistrano.

❋ ***Tico and the Golden Wings***
by Leo Lionni; Knopf 1987. (2-3)
When a wingless bird is granted his wish, his friends
reject him for looking different.

❋ ***King of the Birds***
by Shirley Climo; Harper 1988. (2-3)
The story of how the wren won the honor of being
king and the right to keep all quarreling birds in line.

❋ ***Woodpecker Forest***
by Keizaburo Tejima; Putnam 1989. (2-3)
This tale is about the life of a family of woodpeckers.

❋ ***The Trumpet of the Swan***
by E. B. White; Harper & Row 1970. (4-5)
Louis, a trumpeter swan, is born without a voice and
so he finds a unique way to make himself heard.

❋ ***The Widow and the Parrot***
by Virginia Woolf; Harcourt 1988. (4-5)
A poor widow finds that her miserly brother's
inheritance is a parrot.

❋ ***The Cry of the Crow***
by Jean Craighead George; Harper LB 1980. (5)
Mandy finds a helpless baby crow in the woods and
tries to tame it.

● Non-Fiction ●

LITERATURE SELECTIONS

❋ ***Baltimore Orioles***
by Barbara Brenner; Harper LB 1974. (2)
The yearly life cycle of one oriole family, accurately
and simply described for the beginning reader.

❋ ***Birds***
by Susan Kuchalla; Troll LB 1982. (2-3)
A simple introduction to the many different kinds of
birds.

❋ ***The World of Chickens***
by Jennifer Coldrey; Stevens 1987. (2-4)
Simple text and full-color photos help to explain how
these animals live.

❋ ***The World of Swans***
by Jennifer Coldrey; Stevens 1987. (2-4)
An introduction to the swan for the young reader.

❋ ***Season of the White Stork***
by Heiderose and Andreas Fischer-Nagel; Carolrhoda
1985. (2-5)
Learn about this unusual kind of bird found in
European countries.

❋ ***Birds Do the Strangest Things***
by Leonora Hornblow; Random LB 1965. (2-4)
Find out about unusual birds such as the
hummingbird and the ostrich.

❋ ***Have You Ever Heard of a Kangaroo Bird?***
by Barbara Brenner; Putnam 1980. (3-5)
Meet twenty unusual birds.

❋ ***Birds of Prey***
by Kate Petty; Gloucester 1987. (3-5)
Find out about the hooked beaks, powerful wings and
strong talons on these predator birds.

RELATED STUDIES & ACTIVITY

● Hatching ● Endangered Animals ● Penguins ● Owls ● Animal Habitats ●
● Cut plastic bottles in half to make hanging bird feeders. Record observations of "diners." ●

BIRDS

Title

Author

What kind of bird or birds did you read about?

_____

_____

Pretend you are the bird in the story. Turn the paper over and write a story about a day in your "bird" life.

Choose a bird in the story and write at least three words to describe it.

_____

_____

What did you think was the most interesting thing about a bird in the book?

_____

_____

Describe the home *(habitat)* of one of the birds in the book.

_____

_____

SNAKES

● Fiction ●

LITERATURE SELECTIONS

● *Crictor*
by Romi Ungerer; Harper LB 1958. (2)
A boa constrictor becomes the hero of a small French town after he captures a burglar.

● *The Day Jimmy's Boa Ate the Wash*
by Trinka Hakes Noble; Dial 1980. (2)
A wild class trip to a farm sets off a chain of silly disasters when a student brings his boa constrictor.

● *The Snake That Went to School*
by Lilian Moore; Scholastic 1987. (2-3)
Hank's pet hognose snake, Puffy, disappears from its cage when he takes it to school.

● *Wally*
by Judie Wolkoff; Bradbury 1977. (3-4)
Michael agrees to reptile-sit his friend's pet chuckwalla for two weeks.

● *Harvey's Horrible Snake Disaster*
by Eth. Clifford; Houghton Mifflin 1984. (3-4)
Harvey's lying cousin Nora starts off her annual two-month visit by stealing Slider, a hognose snake.

● *Alice and the Boa Constrictor*
by Laurie Adams; Houghton 1983. (3-5)
A fourth grader is disappointed in her new pet—a boa constrictor.

● *Pearl's Promise*
by Frank Asch; Dell 1984. (4-5)
A mouse named Pearl sets out to save her brother from a pet-store python.

● *Yowder and the Train Robbers*
by Glen Rounds; Holiday House 1981. (4-5)
The unperturbable sign painter foils dangerous outlaws with the help of cooperative rattlesnakes.

● Non-Fiction ●

LITERATURE SELECTIONS

● *Snakes Are Hunters*
by Patricia Lauber; Harper 1988. (2)
This book focuses on how snakes hunt and devour their food.

● *Snakes*
by Ray Broekel; Childrens LB 1982. (2-4)
An introduction to snakes for the primary grades.

● *Reptiles Do the Strangest Things*
by Leonora Hornblow; Random LB 1970. (2-4)
A description of the major reptiles and their living habits.

● *Reptiles*
by Lois Ballard; Childrens 1982. (2-4)
A straightforward, logically arranged introduction.

● *Pythons and Boas*
by Lionel Bender; Gloucester 1988. (3-4)
A look at these fascinating, but often feared snakes.

● *Snakes: Their Place in the Sun*
by Robert M. McClung; Garrard LB 1979. (3-5)
The structure and life cycle of the snake are covered in this introductory account.

● *A Snake's Body*
by Joanna Cole; Morrow LB 1981. (3-5)
An exploration of the body and living habits of the six-foot python.

● *Discovering Snakes and Lizards*
by Neil Curtis; Watts 1986. (4-5)
The reptile world comes to life with color photos and clear text.

RELATED STUDIES & ACTIVITY

● Predator/Prey ● Crocodiles ● Deserts ● Jungles ● Lizards ● Measurement ●
● Stuff dad's tie to make a colorful snake to write about. ●

SNAKES

Title

Author

Describe yourself …
… from the point of view of the snake in the story.

What do you like to eat?

What do you look like?

Where do you live?

What words describe how you move?

What do you do all day?

What problems do you have (or do you cause)?

THE ZOO

• Fiction •
LITERATURE SELECTIONS

❋ *Sam Who Never Forgets*
by Eve Rice; Greenwillow LB 1977. (2)
Sam, the zookeeper, feeds the animals each day, but one day there appears to be nothing for the elephant.

❋ *Encore for Eleanor*
by Bill Peet; Houghton 1981. (2)
After being sent to the zoo, a retired circus elephant learns how to draw and become a star once more.

❋ *If I Ran the Zoo*
by Dr. Seuss; Random House 1950. (2)
Lots of looney animals in rhyme with many colorful illustrations.

❋ *Leo and Emily's Zoo*
by Franz Brandenberg; Greenwillow LB 1988. (2-3)
Lou and Emily stage a backyard zoo to earn money for a visit to a real one.

❋ *Cam Jansen and the Mystery at the Monkey House*
by David A. Adler; Viking 1985. (3-4)
Cam, Eric, and Billy are out to solve the disappearance of monkeys from the zoo.

❋ *Zucchini*
by Barbara Dana; Harper LB 1982. (3-5)
The story of a ferret and his escape from the Bronx Zoo.

❋ *Son for a Day*
by Corinne Gerson; Scholastic 1982. (4-5)
Eleven-year-old Danny finds he can be easily "adopted" by families when he visits the Bronx Zoo.

❋ *Morgan's Zoo*
by James Howe; Macmillan 1984. (4-5)
Morgan, a set of twins, and a number of animals band together to save a zoo.

• Non-Fiction •
LITERATURE SELECTIONS

❋ *Popcorn Park Zoo*
by Wendy Pfeffer; Simon & Schuster 1992. (2-3)
Describes Popcorn Park Zoo in New Jersey which rescues and cares for sick, old or abused animals.

❋ *A Children's Zoo*
by Tana Hoban; Greenwillow LB 1985. (2-3)
Appealing portraits of eleven common zoo animals.

❋ *Zoos*
by Karen Jacobsen; Childrens LB 1982. (2-4)
A very general introduction to zoos with simple language and large color photographs.

❋ *New Zoos*
by Madelyn Klein Anderson; Watts 1987. (3-5)
Describing the trends toward more open and natural environments in zoos.

❋ *Andy Bear: A Polar Cub Grows Up at the Zoo*
by Ginny Johnston/J. Cutchins; Morrow 1985. (2-3)
A zookeeper rescued then raised a bear cub for five months in her own apartment.

❋ *Zoos and Game Reserves*
by Miles Barton; Gloucester 1988. (4-5)
A look at conditions in zoos in this focus on wildlife that is threatened by dangerous environments.

❋ *Behind the Scenes at the Zoo*
by David Paige; Whitman LB 1987. (5)
How zoos initiate and carry out the best care possible for their charges.

❋ *Zoos Without Cages*
by Judith Rinard; National Geographic LB 1981. (5)
Explore zoos where the enclosures are like natural habitats.

RELATED STUDIES & ACTIVITY

• Animals • Birds • Zoo Careers • Animal Habitats • Endangered Species •
• Work cooperatively to create dioramas showing animals in their zoo habitat. •

Title

THE ZOO

Author

Use a Venn diagram to show how the lives of the animals in the zoo you read about are the same and how they are different from animals in their natural habitat.

Think about things such as what they eat, who takes care of them, how they protect themselves, what animals they have contact with and what people they see.

ZOO

BOTH

NATURAL HABITAT

LITERATURE SELECTIONS

● *Frog Odyssey*
by Juliet Snape; Simon & Schuster 1992. (2)
When construction rigs threaten their habitat, a band of tiny green frogs search for a new home.

● *The Princess and the Frog*
by A. Vesey; Little Brown 1985. (2)
An adaptation of the fairy tale in which a princess meets a frog who is actually a prince.

● *It's Mine*
by Leo Lionni; Knopf LB. 1986 (2)
Three griping frogs realize that sharing is better than fighting whan a storm threatens their home.

● *Bullfrog Grows Up*
by Rosamond Dauer; Dell 1988. (2-4)
A frog is befriended by two mice and taken from its pond to their home.

● *Friend or Frog*
by Marjorie Priceman; Houghton 1989. (2-4)
Kate and Hilgon, the frog, go together on a search for his new home.

● *Fish is Fish*
by Leo Lionni; Pantheon 1970. (2-3)
A fable about a fish who learns from a frog how to be happy just being himself.

● *The Frog Prince Continued*
by Jon Scieszka; Viking 1991. (2-3)
What happened after the princess married the frog? He kept acting like a frog, that's what!

● *The Wind in the Willows*
by Kenneth Grahame; Macmillan 1983. (4-5)
An award-winning fantasy involving Toad of Toad Hall.

LITERATURE SELECTIONS

● *Tadpole and Frog*
by Christine Back; Silver LB 1986. (2-3)
When construction rigs threaten their habitat, a band of tiny green frogs search for a new home.

● *Discovering Frogs*
by Douglas Florian; Macmillan 1986. (2-3)
Watercolor sketches enhance this book of the life cycle and characteristics of frogs.

● *Frogs*
by Chris Henwood; Watts 1989. (2-3)
Basic facts about catching and caring for frogs.

● *Why Frogs are Wet*
by Judy Hawes; Harper 1968. (2-3)
Tells about the life of frogs and their history back to prehistoric times.

● *The Complete Frog: A Guide for the Naturalist*
by Christopher Santoro; Lothrop 1989. (3-5)
An introduction to such weather phenomena as snow rain and clouds.

● *The World of Frogs*
by Jennifer Coldrey; Stevens LB 1986. (2-4)
Physical characteristics, habitat and life-style of the frog are the focus of this book.

● *Discovering Frogs and Toads*
by Mike Linley; Watts LB 1986. (4-5)
How frogs and toads live, eat, reproduce and care for their young.

● *The Frog in the Pond*
by Jennifer Coldrey; Stevens LB 1986. (4-5)
Physical characteristics and habitat, with a focus on transformation of tadpole to frog.

RELATED STUDIES & ACTIVITY

● Toads ● Animal habitats ● Water lilies ● Amphibians ● Reptiles ●
● Find out how far frogs can jump; Then have a jumping contest. ●

Describe the *habitat* (home) of the frog in the story.

_____

_____

_____

_____

If you could ask the frog in the story (or a frog in a pond) three questions, what would they be?

_____

_____

_____

FROGS

Title _____

Author _____

_____

_____

Write three facts about frogs (non-fiction books) OR three things that would describe the frog in the story.

_____

_____

_____

How are frogs (or the frog character) in the book different from other animals? _____

_____

_____

● Fiction ●

LITERATURE SELECTIONS

❋ *Tacky the Penguin*
by Helen Lester; Houghton 1988. (2-3)
Most penguins wear black, but Tacky prefers
Hawaiian shirts and checked bow ties.

❋ *The Penguin That Hated the Cold*
by Barbara Brenner; Random House 1973. (2-3)
Tired of being cold, Pablo the penguin decides to
move from the South Pole to a warmer climate.

❋ *Little Penguin's Tale*
by Audrey Wood; Harcourt Brace 1972. (2-3)
Join a penguin in his adventures searching for fun in
a snowy polar world.

❋ *Bibi Takes Flight*
by Michael Gay; Morrow Junior Books 1988. (2-4)
A young penguin resolves to learn how to fly instead
of swim in the cold ocean.

❋ *Penguin Pete*
by Marcus Pfister; Henry Holt 1987. (3-4)
Pete has a good time playing with his fellow birds
and learning to swim in the sea.

❋ *A Tale of Antarctica*
by Ulco Glimmerveen; Scholastic 1989. (3-5)
Penguin environment is threatened by pollution from
man's presence.

❋ *Peter Penguin & the Polar Sea*
by Harry Obedin; Parenting Press 1989. (3-4)
The adventures of a penguin as he explores and plays
in the polar sea.

❋ *Mr. Popper's Penguins*
by Richard & Florence Atwater; Little 1938. (4-5)
Mr. Popper has to get a penguin from the zoo to keep
his homesick penguin company; soon there are 12.

● Non-Fiction ●

LITERATURE SELECTIONS

❋ *The Penguin*
by Paula Z. Hogan; Raintree 1979. (2-3)
For very young readers, an account that has
marvelous illustrations.

❋ *The Penguins in the Snow*
by Douglas Allen; G. Stevens 1988. (2-4)
Penguins feed, breed and defend themselves in their
natural habitat.

❋ *A Penguin Year*
by Susan Bonners; Delacorte LB 1981. (2-4)
An introduction to the life-style of penguins of the
South Pole.

❋ *Penguins*
by Jennifer Coldrey; Andre Deutsch 1984. (2-4)
Following a factual introduction, there is a delightful
album of color photographs.

❋ *The Penguins*
by Lynn M. Stone; Crestwood House 1987. (3-4)
Examines the habitat and physical features of the
emperor penguin.

❋ *Penguin*
by Vincent Serventy; Raintree 1985. (4-5)
Describes the life and habitat of penguins in their
struggle for survival.

❋ *Penguins*
by Cousteau Society; Simon & Schuster 1991. (4-5)
An introduction to the features of this unusual Artic
animal.

❋ *Penguins*
by Sylvia A. Johnson; Lerner LB 1981. (4-5)
Handsome photographs enliven the text of this
introduction to penguins and their habitats.

RELATED STUDIES & ACTIVITY

● Antartica ● Birds ● Habitats ● Adaptation ●

● Form cooperative groups to research and report on different penguins. ●

PENGUINS

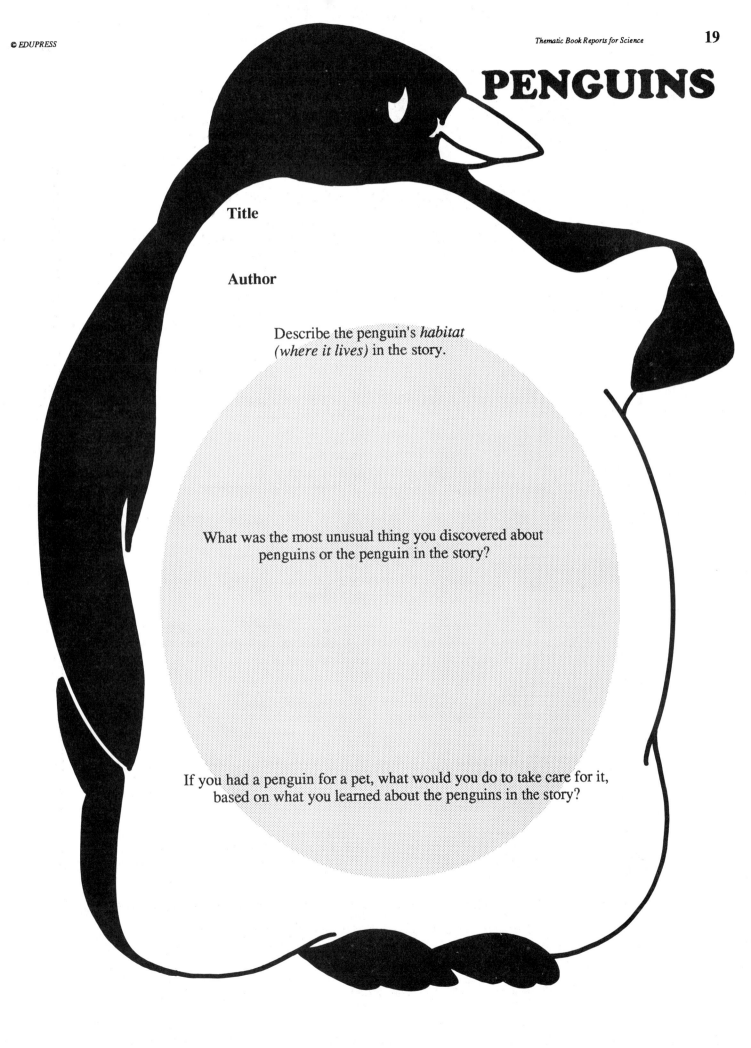

Title

Author

Describe the penguin's *habitat (where it lives)* in the story.

What was the most unusual thing you discovered about penguins or the penguin in the story?

If you had a penguin for a pet, what would you do to take care for it, based on what you learned about the penguins in the story?

ENDANGERED ANIMALS

● Fiction ●

LITERATURE SELECTIONS

❀ In Search of the Last Dodo
by Reg Cartwright; Joy Street Bks 1989. (2-3)
Who will get to the last Dodo egg first—a kindly sea captain or Greedy King Glut?

❀ Tigress
by Helen Cowcher; Farrar, Strauss 1992. (2-3)
When a tigress and her cubs threaten a nearby herd, the ranger devises a plan for a peaceful resolution.

❀ Sally and the Limpet
by Simon James; McElderry Books 1992. (2-3)
Sally pries a limpet off an ocean rock then doesn't know how to get it loose.

❀ Panda
by Susan Bonners; Delacorte 1978. (2-3)
Charming watercolor illustrations accompanying solid information about these mammals from China.

❀ Hugh Pine
by J. Van de Wetering; Houghton 1983. (3-4)
An intelligent Maine porcupine tries to save his fellow porcupines from getting killed by cars.

❀ The Invisible Hunters
by Harriet Rohmer; Children's 1987. (3-4)
The Miskito Indians promise the magical Dar Vine that they will never sell the animals they hunt.

❀ The Absolutely Perfect Horse
by Marylois Dunn & A. Mayhar; Harper 1989. (5)
Annie purchases a broken-down Indian pony to save him from destruction.

❀ Grishka and the Bear
by Rene Guillot; Harper 1960. (5)
The haunting story of a Siberian boy and his bear cub who escape to avoid being sacrificed by villagers.

● Non-Fiction ●

LITERATURE SELECTIONS

❀ Extremely Weird Endangered Species
by Sarah Lovett; John Muir Pub. 1992. (2-3)
Profiles the characteristics and behavior of some of the world's most bizzare endangered species.

❀ Danger on the Arctic Ice
by Elisabeth Sackett; Sierra 1991. (2-3)
A dramatic story of young animals in the perilous arctic ice and their fight for survival.

❀ Danger on the African Grassland
by Elisabeth Sackett; Sierra 1991. (2-3)
A handsome and informative story of the fragile and threatened ecologies of the African Grasslands.

❀ Catskill Eagle
by Herman Melville; Putnam 1991. (2-4)
Explore the world of the majestic mountain eagle in a tribute to the struggles of an endangered species.

❀ Animals in Danger
by William McCay; Aladdin 1992. (3-4)
Pop-up book brings eight endangered animals to three dimensional life.

❀ As Dead as a Dodo
by Paul Rice; Godine 1981. (4-5)
An examination of many animals that are extinct and why they disappeared.

❀ Bringing Back the Animals
by Teresa Kinnedy; Amethyst 1991. (4-5)
A study of endangered species discusses efforts to protect and restore twelve endangered animals.

❀ And Then There Was One: The Mysteries of Extinction
by Margery Facklam; Sierra Book Clubs 1990. (4-5)
A survey of the causes and victims of extinction.

RELATED STUDIES & ACTIVITY

● Rain Forest ● Animal Habitats ● Conservation ● Ecology ● Ocean Life ●
● Add articles and stories to a classroom scrapbook of endangered species. ●

Endangered Animals

Title

Author

Describe the habitat of an endangered animal in the book.

What is happening that is putting this animal in danger?

How does the animal you read about get its food?

What would you do, that is different from what you read about, to help this endangered animal?

Write your thoughts on another paper.

What is being done to help this animal?

● Fiction ●

LITERATURE SELECTIONS

❋ *Clementina's Cactus*
by Ezra Jack Keats; Viking 1982. (2)
A young girl is curious about a cactus plant she sees.

❋ *Abdul*
by Rosemary Wells; Dial 1975. (2)
Gilda, a camel, gives birth to Abdul, who strangely
resembles a horse.

❋ *Cactus Hotel*
by Brenda Z. Guiberson; Holt 1992. (2-3)
A Gila woodpecker comes to eat then decides to stay.
He has found the perfect place to begin a new hotel.

❋ *How the Camel Got His Hump*
by Rudyard Kipling; Bedrick 1985. (2-4)
Find out the possible solution in this retelling of
Rudyard Kipling's classic tale.

❋ *The Adventures of Agnes, a Camel, & Her Good
   Friend Shopworth*
by Hannah Klein; Vantage 1991. (3-4)
These two friends pack adventure into their lives.

❋ *Hawk, I'm Your Brother*
by Byrd Baylor; Macmillan LB 1976. (3-5)
A desert boy captures a young hawk, hoping it will
teach him how to fly.

❋ *Pamela Camel*
by Bill Peet; Houghton Mifflin 1986. (4-5)
Pamela may be the most unusual camel you'll ever
meet. Find out why!

❋ *Medicine Walk*
by Ardath Mayhar; Macmillan 1985. (5)
A boy survives a plane crash and must make his way
out of the desert with skills learned from an Apache.

● Non-Fiction ●

LITERATURE SELECTIONS

❋ *Desert Year*
by Carol Lerner; Morrow 1991. (2)
Reveal how plants and animals of the desert adapt to
their environment, in a study of an American desert.

❋ *The Desert Is Theirs*
by Byrd Baylor; Aladdin 1991. (2-3)
Learn about desert flora and fauna and the Desert
People who know its secrets.

❋ *Mojave*
by Diane Siebert; HarperCollins 1992. (2-3)
Paintings and text capture the landscape and
inhabitants of the harsh Mojave Desert.

❋ *Deserts*
by Seymour Simon; Morrow 1990. (2-3)
Looks at different types of deserts and explains how
plants and animals survive in this harsh environment.

❋ *Desert Giant: The World of the Saguaro Cactus*
by Barbara Bash; Sierra Club 1989. (3-4)
How the Sonoran desert cactus grows, and after 150
years, flowers and bears fruit.

❋ *Camels: Ships of the Desert*
by John F. Waters; Crowell 1974. (4-5)
The focus is on the camel's unique ability to adapt to
desert existence.

❋ *Cactus*
by Cynthia Overbeck; Lerner LB 1982. (3-5)
A description of the cactus and how it lives in its dry
environment.

❋ *A Night and Day in the Desert*
by Jennifer Dewey; Little, Brown 1991. (4-5)
A look at the many forms of life existing in the
austere desert environment.

RELATED STUDIES & ACTIVITY

● Deserts ● Temperature ● Survival ● Animal Habitats ● Lizards ●

● Divide into cooperative groups and have each research a different desert. ●

Write a travel guide for a desert traveller.
Provide information based on the book you read.

Desert Guide Book

Animals You Will See	**Plants You Will See**
Interesting animal fact:	*Interesting plant fact:*
Weather Conditions	**Things You'll Want To Photograph**
Ways to adapt:	*Something funny or fascinating:*

Cactus & Camels

Title

Author

PLANETS

● Fiction ●

LITERATURE SELECTIONS

❂ ***The Magic School Bus***
by Joanna Cole; Scholastic 1990. (2)
Ms. Frizzle's class takes a field trip into outer space
and visits each planet in the solar system.

❂ ***Guys from Space***
by Daniel Pinkwater; Macmillan 1989. (2)
Aliens land in a boy's back yard and take him for a
ride to a planet with talking blue rocks.

❂ ***My Trip to Alpha I***
by Alfred Slote Lippincott 1978. (3-4)
In the sophisticated future, Jack visits his aunt on
another planet via VOYA-CODE body travel.

❂ ***The Wonderful Flight to the Mushroom Planet***
by Eleanor Cameron; Little 1954. (4-5)
The story of two boys who take off on a spaceship
with a magical man named Tyco Bass.

❂ ***Matthew Looney's Invasion of the Earth***
by Jerome Beatty; Harper & Row 1965. (4-5)
An adventure-prone Moon boy joins an earthbound
expedition searching for intelligent life.

❂ ***The Donkey Planet***
by Scott Corbett; Dutton 1979. (4-5)
Two young scientists must bring back samples of a
metal from another planet.

❂ ***A Wrinkle in Time***
by Madeleine L'Engle; Farrar 1962. (5)
Meg travels through time and space to rescue her
scientist father from the sinister planet of Camazotz.

❂ ***The Green Book***
by Jill Paton Walsh; Farrar 1982. (5)
Patti tells the story of how her family journeys away
from the dying earth to live on another planet.

● Non-Fiction ●

LITERATURE SELECTIONS

❂ ***Saturn***
by Simon Seymour; Morrow LB 1985. (2-4)
Lots of information about Saturn and its rings,
enhanced with color photographs.

❂ ***The Planets in Our Solar System***
by Franklyn M. Branley; Harper LB 1987. (2-4)
This revised edition incorporates our ever-growing
information on the solar system.

❂ ***The Moon Seems to Change***
by Franklyn M. Branley; Harper LB 1987. (2-4)
A clear text that discusses our ever-changing
knowledge and information about the moon.

❂ ***Jupiter***
by Seymour Simon; Morrow LB 1985. (2-4)
A detailed look at Jupiter, enhanced by photographs
taken mostly from unmanned spacecraft.

❂ ***Mars***
by Seymour Simon; Morrow LB 1987. (2-4)
Lucid text and spectacular photos highlight this
detailed study of the Red planet.

❂ ***The Giant Planets***
by Alan E. Nourse; Watts LB 1982. (4-5)
Information on the large planets, plus their formation,
and composition is given.

❂ ***Journey to the Planets***
by Patricia Lauber; Crown 1990. (4-5)
Drawing on recent findings from the Voyager
expedition, a study documents nine planets.

❂ ***Neptune***
by Franklyn M. Branley; HarperCollins 1992. (4-5)
Full-color photographs from Voyager 2 provide a
revealing look at Neptune.

RELATED STUDIES & ACTIVITY

● Astonomy ● Gravity ● Space exploration ● Solar System ●

● Work cooperatively using recycled materials to create a solar system mobile . ●

PLANETS

What is the name of the planet
you visited in your book? Is it real or imaginary?

Title

Author

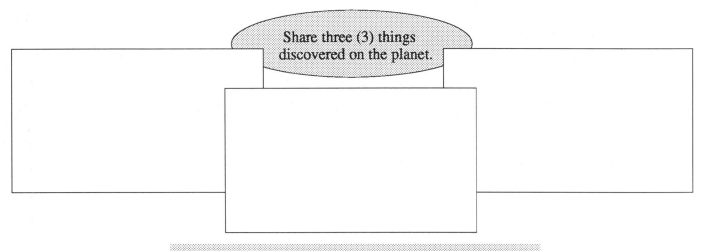

Share three (3) things
discovered on the planet.

Retell four events in the story in the order they happened.

_____

_____

_____

_____

Turn the paper over and draw a picture of a solar system showing the planet or planets visited in the book.

● Fiction ●

LITERATURE SELECTIONS

● *Rain Forest*
by Helen Cowcher; Farrar 1988. (2)
A machine cuts down the trees in the rain forest, and
when the rains come, the river bursts its banks.

● *The Great Kapok Tree*
by Lynne Cherry; Harcourt 1990. (2)
A man falls asleep under a kapok tree in the rain
forest and the creatures beg him not to destroy it.

● *Where the Forest Meets the Sea*
by Jeannie Baker; Greenwillow Books 1987. (2-3)
A young boy pretends it is long ago as he walks
among the trees of an Australian tropical rain forest.

● *Aldita and the Forest*
by Thelma Catterwell; Houghton Mifflin 1989. (2-3)
Newborn butterfly finds herself in an Australian
forest where she learns about "the plan."

● *Amazon Boy*
by Ted Lewin; Macmillan 1992. (3-4)
A Brazilian boy sees firsthand all the wealth the
Amazon River provides for his people.

● *Panther Dream*
by Bob and Wendy Weir; Hyperion 1991. (4-5)
A mysterious black panther shares a special message
about the preservation of the African rain forests.

● *Journey of the Red-Eyed Tree Frog*
by Tanis Jordan; Green Tiger Press 1992. (4-5)
Ronnie, a tiny, red-eyed tree frog, races against time
to stop the destruction of his beloved rain forest.

● *One Day in the Tropical Rainforest*
by Jean Craighead George; HarperCollins 1990. (5)
The future of the rainforest of the macaw depends on
a scientist and a young Indian boy.

● Non-Fiction ●

LITERATURE SELECTIONS

● *Rainforest*
by Barbara Taylor; Houghton Mifflin 1992. (2)
A study of the endangered rain forests describes the
varied lifeforms that make this area their home.

● *Amazon Rainforest*
by Moria Butterfield; Times Four 1991. (2-3)
Beautiful illustrations complemented by a press-out
model jungle brings the rain forest to life.

● *The Jungle*
by Carroll Norden; Raintree LB 1978. (2-4)
Tropical rain forests and their inhabitants are
presented clearly with good illustrations.

● *This Place is Wet*
by Vicki Cobb; Walker 1989. (2-4)
Focuses on the land, ecology, people and animals of
the Amazon rain forest in Brazil.

● *Tracking Wild Chimpanzees in Kirbira National
Park*
by Joyce Powzyk; Lothrop LB 1988. (3-5)
A trip to the rain forest in Burundi, Africa.

● *Endangered Animals of the Rain Forest*
by Sandra Uchitel; Price, Stern, Stoane 1992. (3-5)
Young explorers travel deep into the rain forest to
learn about the majestic mountain gorilla.

● *An Adventure in the Amazon*
by Cousteau Society; Simon & Schuster 1992. (4-5)
Take a journey into the fragile rain forest of the
Amazon.

● *The Rain Forest*
by Billy Goodman; Little, Brown 1992. (4-5)
Examines the wide array of plants and animals living
in rain forests and the dangers threatening them.

RELATED STUDIES & ACTIVITY

● Jungles ● Amazon ● Environment ● Endangered Species ● Pollution ●
● Make a large class mural displaying the layers of the rain forest. ●

RAIN FOREST

Title	**Author**

What special "gifts" does the rain forest share with the people living in it or a character in the story.

_____

_____

Fill in the boxes below. Write a sentence or make a list that describes each category you encountered in your reading.

Animals

People

RAIN FOREST

Plants

CLOUDS

● Fiction ●

LITERATURE SELECTIONS

❀ *It Looked Like Spilt Milk*
by Charles Shaw; Harper & Row 1947. (2)
Cloud-gazing is an obvious follow-up to this simple
white-on-dark-blue depiction of clouds.

❀ *Hi, Clouds*
by Carol Greene; Childrens LB 1983. (2)
Two children see many objects in clouds in this easy-
to-read book.

❀ *The Cloud's Journey*
by Sigrid Heuck; Atomium Bks 1991. (2-3)
Follow the trip of this imaginary cloud, from
formation to storm.

❀ *C.L.O.U.D.S.*
by Pat Cummings; Lothrop 1986. (2-3)
Chuku finds a girl who appreciates his work of
designing the skies in New York City.

❀ *Cloudy with a Chance of Meatballs*
by Judi Barrett; Atheneum 1978. (2-3)
The town of ChewandSwallow undergoes a crisis
when their normal edible weather turns nasty.

❀ *Jonathan's Cloud*
by Gardner McFall; Harper LB 1986. (3-4)
When a cloud floats in his bedroom window,
Jonathan tries to find out how to keep it.

❀ *The Little Cloud That Couldn't*
by Jeanne Arnold; Media Serv. Unltd. 1990. (3-5)
An environmental story about the effects of a cloud
that couldn't rain.

❀ *The Cloud*
by Deborah Kogan Ray; Harper 1984. (4-5)
A little girl struggles to hike up a mountain in hopes
of seeing a beautiful white cloud.

● Non-Fiction ●

LITERATURE SELECTIONS

❀ *Little Dark Cloud*
by Bridget Fitzgerald; Unicorn 1973. (2)
What does it mean when you see a very dark cloud in
the sky? Read and find out!

❀ *Clouds*
by Carol Greene; Childrens 1985. (2)
A simple introduction to the types and names of
clouds we see in the sky.

❀ *The Cloud Book*
by Tomie dePaola; Holiday House 1975. (2-3)
Explanation of all types of clouds including delicious,
long names like cumulonimbus and cirrostratus.

❀ *Storms*
by Seymour Simon; Morrow 1989. (3-5)
Explains how clouds gather and storms occur.

❀ *It's Raining Cats and Dogs: All Kinds of Weather
and Why We Have It*
by Franklyn Branley; Houghton 1987. (3-5)
An account of strange weather happenings and the
role that clouds play in them.

❀ *Weather Watch*
by Adam Ford; Lothrop 1982. (4-5)
A simple introduction to such weather phenomena as
snow, rain and clouds.

❀ *Weather and Its Work*
by David Lambert; Facts on File 1984. (5)
Contains data on thunderstorms, drought and more.

❀ *The Weather Sky*
by Bruce McMillan; Farrar, Strauss 1985. (5)
In-depth exploration of cloud formations and their
effects on weather conditions and changes.

RELATED STUDIES & ACTIVITY

● Weather ● Storms ● Tornadoes ● Water Cycles ● Sky ●

● Make adjective dictionaries that feature a different cloud on each page. ●

CLOUDS

Title

Author

Write at least five words found in your book that describe or name clouds.

What effect did the clouds in the book have on the main character or weather changes—or both?

Imagine the clouds in the book were people. Describe what they see, from their point of view.

● Fiction ●

LITERATURE SELECTIONS

● *An Evening at Alfie's*
by Shirley Hughes; Lothrop 1984. (2)
While Alfie's baby-sitter reads a story, a pipe bursts
in the ceiling, making puddles all over the floor.

● *The Water of Life: A Tale from the Brothers
    Grimm*
by Grimm Brothers; Holiday 1986. (2)
Three brothers search for the water of life.

● *Tattie's River Journey*
by Shirley Murphy; Dial LB 1983. (2-3)
Tattie is caught in a flood and faces many dangers
but, rescues many animals in the process.

● *What Makes Tiddalik Laugh: An Australian
    Aborigine Folktale*
by Joanna Troughton; Bedrick 1986. (2-3)
A giant frog drinks all the water on earth.

● *The Unicorn and the Lake*
by Marianna Mayer; Dial LB 1982. (3-4)
A helpful unicorn purifies a lake so animals may use
it again.

● *Where the River Begins*
by Thomas Locker; Dial LB 1984. (3-4)
Two boys hike with their grandfather to the source of
a river.

● *Llama and the Great Flood*
by Ellen Alexander; Crowell 1989. (3-5)
A Peruvian llama's dream of a five-day flood helps
him save his owner's family.

● *The Magic School Bus at the Waterworks*
by Joanna Cole; Scholastic 1988. (3-5)
Ms. Frizzle takes her class through the clouds, into
the reservoir and out the bathroom sink.

● Non-Fiction ●

LITERATURE SELECTIONS

● *Rain Drop Splash*
by Alvin Tresselt; Lothrop 1946. (2-3)
Explains how raindrops form a puddle that grows
from pond to river and finally joins the sea.

● *Water*
by Alfred Leutscher; Dial 1983. (2-3)
The various forms of water and their importance to
the life support are discussed.

● *Water: What It Is, What It Does*
by Judith S. Seixas; Greenwillow LB 1987. (2-4)
Easy-to-read chapters describe properties and uses of
water and its effects on the environment.

● *What Makes It Rain? The Story of a Raindrop*
by Keith Brandt; Troll 1982. (2-4)
A simple book about the water cycle.

● *Rain Shadow*
by James R. Newton; Harper LB 1983. (3-4)
Explore the land that lies on the leeward side of the
western Cascade mountains.

● *The Trip of a Drip?*
by Vicki Cobb; Little 1986. (3-5)
A clear explanation with many examples and
experiments with water.

● *Water Resources*
by Trudy Hanmer; Watts 1985. (4-5)
Describes where water is found, its uses and misuses
and what is being done today to conserve it.

● *Water for the World*
by Franklyn M. Branley; Harper LB 1982. (5)
Find out about the water cycle and water
conservation.

RELATED STUDIES & ACTIVITY

● Rivers and Lakes ● Rain ● Snow ● Drought ● Water Cycle ● Floods ●
● Make posters that show the water cycle and encourage conservation. ●

WATER

Title _____

Author

_____

In what form was the water
you read about? Describe it.

How did water help or hurt the main character or people in the book?

If you read a fiction book, pretend you are the water. What would you say to the main character?
If you read a non-fiction book, pretend you are a raindrop. Describe your trip through the water cycle.

LITERATURE SELECTIONS

❋ *Squirrel Park*
by Lisa Campbell Ernst; Bradbury Press 1992. (2)
Chuck's best friend is a squirrel whose home—the big old oak tree—is threatened by a builder.

❋ *The Wartville Wizard*
by Don Madden; Macmillan 1986. (2)
An old man who gains the "power over trash" sends back all the town's litter.

❋ *The Wump World*
by Bill Peet; Houghton Mifflin 1974. (2-3)
The usually peaceful Wump planet is invaded by the Pollutians from the planet Pollutus.

❋ *The Forgotten Forest*
by Laurence Anholt; Sierra Club Books 1992. (2-3)
Fable about a country where all but one forest has been cleared for cities—and now that is threatened.

❋ *Trouble at Marsh Harbor*
by Susan Sharpe; Puffin 1992. (3-4)
Ben makes friends with a scientist trying to find the source of an oil leak threatening Chesapeake Bay.

❋ *The Unicorn and the Lake*
by Marianna Mayer; Dial 1982. (3-4)
A helpful unicorn purifies a lake so his animal friends may use it.

❋ *Top Secret*
by John Reynolds Gardner; Little, Brown 1985. (4-5)
Everyone scoffs when a nine-year-old claims to have discovered how to turn sunlight into food.

❋ *Moon-Dark*
by Patricia Wrightson; Macmillan 1988. (5)
Flying foxes, uprooted by humans, raid fruit trees and cause an ecological imbalance.

LITERATURE SELECTIONS

❋ *The Great Kapok Tree: A Tale of the Amazon Rain Forest*
by Lynne Cherry; Harcourt 1990. (2)
Rain forest animals plead their case for conservation.

❋ *A River Ran Wild: An Environmental History*
by Lynne Cherry; Harcourt 1992. (2-3)
The "life" story of a river and the effects of time and change.

❋ *Pioneer of Ecology*
by Rachel Carson; Puffin 1992. (3-4)
Carson's biography shares with readers her great interest in the environment.

❋ *Save the Earth*
by Betty Miles; Knopf 1991. (3-5)
Provides readers with timely information about environmental problems and how to solve them.

❋ *Going Green: A Kid's Handbook to Saving the Planet*
by John Elkington; Puffin 1992. (4-5)
Useful suggestions for improving our immediate environment.

❋ *Come Back, Salmon*
by Molly Come; Little, Brown 1992. (4-5)
The inspiring story of how a dedicated group of school children adopted a stream and rescued it.

❋ *Space Junk: Pollution Beyond the Earth*
by Judy Donnelly; Morrow 1990. (4-5)
Explains how environmental destruction threatens our future and what we can do to prevent catastrophe.

❋ *The Glass Ark*
by Linnea Gentry; Puffin 1992. (5)
The story of Biosphere 2, the world's biggest greenhouse where scientists will live for two years.

RELATED STUDIES & ACTIVITY

● Trees ● Recycling ● Environment ● Conservation ● Pollution ● Rain Forest ●
● Have a clean-up day. Weigh how many pounds of debris are collected. ●

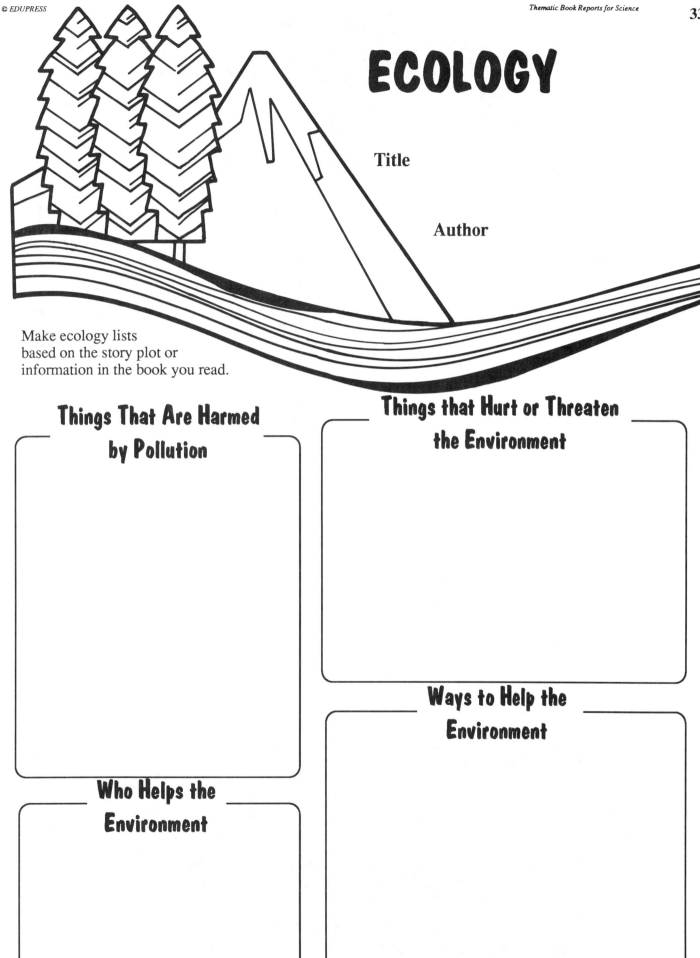

ECOLOGY

Title

Author

Make ecology lists
based on the story plot or
information in the book you read.

Things That Are Harmed by Pollution

Things that Hurt or Threaten the Environment

Ways to Help the Environment

Who Helps the Environment

LITERATURE SELECTIONS

● *Under the Sun*
by Ellen Kandoian; Dodd, Mead 1987. (2)
Molly's mother gives her the answer to the question of where the sun goes at night.

● *Sun's Up*
by Teryl Euvremer; Crown 1987. (2)
Sun goes about the day's business, from waking up the earth to painting rainbows.

● *Why the Sun and Moon Live in the Sky*
by Elphinstone Dayrell; Houghton Mifflin 1990. (2)
An African folktale that attempts to explain sky phenomena.

● *The Perfect Mouse*
by Dick Gackenbach; Macmillan 1984. (2-3)
Two social-climbing mice want their daughter to marry the sun.

● *Under the Green Willow*
by Elizabeth Coatsworth; Greenwillow 1984. (2-3)
The sun describes a place where a variety of animals await food.

● *Where Does the Sun Go at Night*
by Mirra Ginsburg; Greenwillow LB 1980. (2-4)
A question-and-answer format is used in this adaptation of an Armenian song.

● *The Miser Who Wanted the Sun*
by Jurg Obrist; Macmillan 1984. (3-4)
A miser commissions a tailor to produce a golden robe so he will be like the sun.

● *Brother Mouky and the Falling Sun*
by Karen Whiteside; Harper LB 1980. (3-5)
Mouky is angry with his brother and does not want to resolve the problem.

LITERATURE SELECTIONS

● *The Sun: Our Nearest Star*
by Franklyn M. Branley; Harper LB 1988. (2-3)
An easily read book about the sun and its importance in our lives.

● *Sun Up, Sun Down*
by Gail Gibbons; Harcourt 1983. (2-3)
An introductory account of the sun and its effects on earth.

● *The Sun*
by Kate Petty; Watts 1985. (2-4)
Large-print, simle text and color photos help to introduce the earth's most important star.

● *Eclipse: Darkness in Daytime*
by Franklyn M. Branley; Harper LB 1988. (2-4)
A clear explanation of the total solar eclipse phenomenon.

● *The Sun: Our Very Own Star*
by Jeanne Bendick; Millbrook 1991. (3-4)
A fact-filled study of the sun, its characteristics and its role in the solar system.

● *Sunshine Makes the Seasons*
by Franklyn M. Branley; Harper 1988. (3-4)
An explanation of the seasons by exploring the relationship of the sun to the earth and its orbit.

● *The Sun*
by Heather Couper/Nigel Henbest; Watts 1986 (3-5)
Inviting format and illustrations highlight this introduction to the earth's most important star.

● *The Sun: Our Neighborhood Star*
by David Darling; Dillon 1984. (3-5)
One in a series designed to give young readers a sense of earth's place in the universe.

RELATED STUDIES & ACTIVITY

● Moon ● Stars ● Clouds ● Sky ● Weather ●
● Challenge cooperative groups to design and make a replica of the sun. ●

Title _____   **Author** _____

Pretend you are the sun in the story. Describe yourself.

_____

_____

_____

Why was the sun important in the story?
If you read a non-fiction book, how is the sun important to the earth?

_____

_____

_____

If the sun you read about were a person, how would you describe its personality? Why?

_____

_____

_____

VOLCANOES

● Fiction ●

LITERATURE SELECTIONS

● *Fountain of Fire*
by Gill McBarn; Ruwanga 1987. (2)
Is it a fountain or is it a volcano? Or both? Visit an
erupting volcano.

● *Hill of Fire*
by Thomas P. Lewis; Harper & Row 1971. (2)
An ordinary Mexican farmer discovers a volcano
growing in his cornfield.

● *The Ponies of Mykillengi*
by Lonzo Anderson; Scribner 1966. (2-3)
After an earthquake and a volcano erupts, two
siblings witness their pony giving birth.

● *The Magic School Bus Inside the Earth*
by Joanna Cole; Scholastic 1987. (2-4)
Ms. Frizzle's crew digs right through the Earth,
identifying sedimentary and metamorphic rocks.

● *The Village of Round and Square Houses*
by Ann Grifalconi; Little, Brown 1986. (2-4)
The story of the West African village of Tos and the
eruption of Old Naka long ago.

● *The Finches' Fabulous Furnace*
by Roger Drury; Little, Brown 1971. (4-5)
The Finch family discovers that having a volcano,
even a small one, makes for hilarious misadventures.

● *The Twenty-One Balloons*
by William Pene du Bois; Viking 1947. (5)
Professor Sherman provides a detailed account of his
fantastic balloon voyage to the island of Krakatoa.

● *Paul's Volcano*
by Beatrice Gormley; Houghton 1987. (5)
Adam and new kid, Paul, tangle over a science-fair
volcano model that seems to have its own mind.

● Non-Fiction ●

LITERATURE SELECTIONS

● *Volcanoes*
by Seymour Simon; Morrow 1988. (2)
Provides a close-up look at four major types of
volcanoes and explains their origins and processes.

● *Pompeii … Buried Alive!*
by Edith Kunhardt; Random House 1987. (2-3)
The ancient city of Pompeii and its inhabitants are
completely buried when a volcano erupts.

● *Volcanoes*
by Seymour Simon; Morrow LB 1988. (2-3)
How volcanoes are formed and erupt, with well-
known examples.

● *Volcano: The Eruption and Healing of Mount St.
Helens*
by Patricia Lauber; Aladdin 1992. (2-4)
Relive the 1980 eruption of Mount St. Helens.

● *Volcano*
by Lionel Bender; Watts 1988. (4-5)
Different types of volcanoes throughout the world.

● *The Eruption of Krakatoa*
by Matthews Rupert; Watts 1989. (3-5)
When a dormant volcano on Krakatoa comes to life
again, the results are disastrous.

● *Pompeii: Nightmare at Midday*
by Kathryn Humphrey; Watts 1990. (4-5)
Relive the devastation of the volcano that destroyed
the city of Pompeii.

● *Surtsey: The Newest Place on Earth*
by Kathryn Lasky; Hyperion 1992. (4-5)
On November 14, 1963, a volcanic mountain rose
from the sea. The Icelandic people named it Sursey.

RELATED STUDIES & ACTIVITY

● Earthquakes ● Erosion ● Mountains ● Lava ● Rocks ● Natural Disasters ●
● Go on a hike to hunt for rocks with properties similar to lava. ●

VOLCANOES

Title   **Author**

Pretend you are a newspaper reporter who has been assigned the job of covering the story of the volcanic eruption you read about. A good reporter would include this information …

Where was the volcano located? What was the date?

What sights and sounds were seen and heard?

Were people hurt? What damage was there to homes and towns?

What happened to plants, trees and animals?

● Fiction ●

LITERATURE SELECTIONS

● The Plant Sitter
by Gene Zion; Harper LB 1959. (2)
Tommy learns a lot when he volunteers to take care of the neighbor's plants.

● Petranella
by Betty Waterton; Vanguard 1981. (2)
A pioneer girl loses the flower seeds her grandmother gave her before the family sailed to North America.

● The Great Green Turkey Creek Monster
by James Flora; Atheneum 1976. (2-3)
The almost unstoppable Great Green Hooligan Vine escapes and overtakes the town.

● Miss Rumphius
by Barbara Cooney; Puffin 1982. (2-3)
Miss Rumphius sows flower seeds along the seacoast where she lives in a pledge to make the world better.

● Rotten Island
by William Steig; Godine 1984. (2-3)
A flower appears on an island populated with thorny plants and monsters and sets off a brawl.

● The Poppy Seed
by Clyde Robert Bulla; Harper 1955. (2-4)
A young Indian boy in Mexico plants poppy seeds throughout the village.

● The Star Maiden: An Ojibway Tale
by Barbara Juster Esbensen; Little, Brown 1988. (3-5)
A glowing star longs to live among people as a flower, which is how water lilies came to be.

● Top Secret
by John Reynolds Gardiner; Little Brown 1985. (5)
Allen pursues his science project of human photosynthesis until he turns into a plantlike boy.

● Non-Fiction ●

LITERATURE SELECTIONS

● Plants in Winter
by Joanna Cole; Harper LB 1973. (2-3)
Learn how plants have adapted to winter conditions in order to survive.

● Dandelion
by Barrie Watts; Silver LB 1987. (2-3)
The simple dandelion in close-up photography.

● Weeds and Wildflowers
by Illa Podendorf; Childrens LB 1981. (2-3)
Explore the varied world of plants and flowers that grow wild.

● Cactus
by Cynthia Overbeck; Lerner LB 1982. (3-5)
A description of the cactus and how it manages to live in its arid environment.

● Flowers for You: Blooms for Every Month
by Anita Holmes; Bradbury Press 1992. (3-5)
Learn basic plant care information and how-to tips about twelve flowering plants.

● Sunflowers
by Cynthia Overbeck; Lerner LB 1981. (4-5)
An excellently illustrated introduction to the beautiful and useful plant.

● Carnivorous Plants
by Cynthia Overbeck; Lerner 1982. (4-5)
Learn about plants that "dine" on insects in order to survive in nutrient-poor soil.

● More Plants That Changed History
by Joan Elma Rahn; Macmillan 1985. (5)
A look at five plants that changed history—grains, spices, sugar, potatoes and even coal.

RELATED STUDIES & ACTIVITY

● Seeds ● Photosynthesis ● Sunlight ● Pollination ● Bulbs ●

● Find out about a plant or flower that grows in the area where you live. ●

PLANTS

Title _____   **Author** _____

Write three words that would describe the plant or flower you read about.

_____

Pretend you are the plant in the book. Look around and describe where you live.

_____

_____

_____

How did the plant affect or change the lives of people around it?

_____

_____

_____

What was special or different about the plant you read about?

_____

_____

_____

Turn the paper over and draw a picture of a plant in the book.

❖ Fiction ❖

LITERATURE SELECTIONS

❖ *Cyrus the Unsinkable Sea Serpent*
by Bill Peet; Houghton Mifflin 1975. (2)
A peaceful sea monster sets out to wreck a ship, but
ends up protecting it from ocean disasters.

❖ *Demetrius and the Golden Goblet*
by Eve Bunting; Harcourt 1980. (2-3)
A prince and a sponge diver have different attitudes
about the sea.

❖ *The King's Stilts*
by Dr. Seuss; Random House 1930. (2-3)
Eric returns the king's stilts in time to save the
kingdom from a threatening ocean.

❖ *I Was All Thumbs*
by Bernard Waber; Houghton Mifflin 1975. (2-3)
Legs, the Octopus, must learn to adapt and make new
friends after being released into the sea.

❖ *Very First Last Time*
by Jan Andrews; McElderry 1986. (2-3)
An eerie story about a girl's first trip under the sea to
gather mussels for her family to eat for a winter meal.

❖ *Why the Tides Ebb and Flow*
by Joan Bowden; Houghton Mifflin 1979. (2-5)
Old woman takes the rock from the bottom of the sea
and water begins to pour through the bottomless hole.

❖ *Call It Courage*
by Armstrong Sperry; Macmillan 1940. (4-5)
Polynesian chief's son sets out alone in a canoe to
overcome his fear of the sea in order to be accepted.

❖ *The Black Pearl*
by Scott O'Dell; Houghton Mifflin 1967. (5)
Ramon recalls his life-and-death struggles while
seeking a pearl from an undersea monster.

❖ Non-Fiction ❖

LITERATURE SELECTIONS

❖ *Nature Hide & Seek: Oceans*
by John Norris Wood; Random House 1985. (2-3)
A description of the plants and animals that live on
the bottom of the ocean.

❖ *The Atlantic Ocean*
by Susan Heinrichs; Childrens 1986. (2-4)
An introduction to the Atlantic—shorelines, currents,
flora and fauna.

❖ *The Pacific Ocean*
by Susan Heinrichs; Childrens 1986. (2-4)
An introduction to the world's largest ocean—
shorelines, currents, flora and fauna.

❖ *Life in the Oceans*
by Norbert Wu; Little, Brown 1991. (3-5)
A simple account of oceans and ocean life.

❖ *Fish (Eyewitness Books)*
by Steve Parker; Random House 1990. (3-5)
Photographs and text explore the characteristics,
habitats and varieties of fish and undersea life.

❖ *Thor Heyerdahl: Across the Seas of Time*
by Paul Westman; Dillon LB 1982. (3-5)
The story of the determined contemporary explorer
and his adventure.

❖ *Tales from the South Pacific*
by Anne Gittins; Stemmer 1977. (4-5)
Twenty-two folktales in which the sea and its
creatures play important roles.

❖ *Kon-Tiki: A True Adventure of Survival at Sea*
by Thor Heyerdahl; Washington Sq. Pr. 1984. (4-5)
An adventurous story about the recreation of a raft
trip across the ocean.

RELATED STUDIES & ACTIVITY

❖ Whales ❖ Sharks ❖ Sea Life ❖ Ocean Habitats ❖ Submarines ❖ Shells ❖
❖ Paint a classroom mural that includes plants, animals and other ocean life. ❖

THE OCEAN

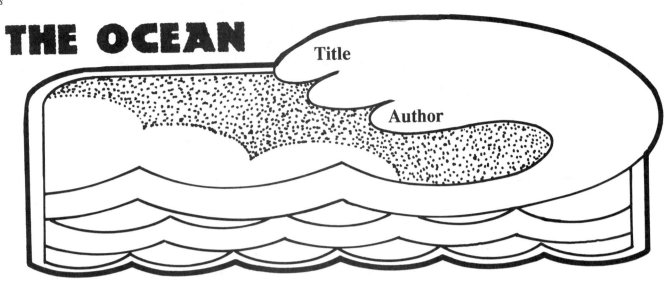

Title

Author

Write five words that would describe the ocean you read about in the book.

Tell about an event or adventure that happened in the story. How did the ocean play a part?

What was the most interesting thing about the ocean you learned in the book?

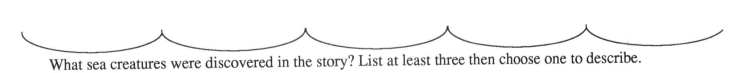

What sea creatures were discovered in the story? List at least three then choose one to describe.

LITERATURE SELECTIONS

❂ How the Whale Got His Throat
by Rudyard Kipling; Peter Bedrick 1987. (2)
A small fish convinces a whale to eat a shipwrecked
mariner, who puts an end to the whale's appetite.

❂ Burt Dow, Deep-Water Man
by Robert McCloskey; Viking 1963. (2-3)
The humorous tale of an old fisherman who catches a
whale by the tale then covers the hole with a bandage.

❂ Whales: The Gentle Giants
by Joyce Milton; Random 1989. (2-3)
A sailor named Brendan steps on the back of a whale
and takes an adventurous ride.

❂ John Tabor's Ride
by Edward C. Day; Knopf LB 1989. (2-3)
The tale of John Tabor and his magical ride around
the world on a whale.

❂ Amos and Boris
by William Steig; Farrar 1971. (2)
The story of a friendship between Amos, a seafaring
mouse, and Boris, his whale rescuer.

❂ Whale in the Sky
by Anne Siberell; Dutton 1982. (2-3)
A legend about Thunderbird who removes Whale
from the sea to save the salmon for the Indians.

❂ Demo and the Dolphin
by Nathaniel Benchley; Harper LB. (4-5)
A young boy and his dolphin visit the site of ancient
Greece.

❂ The Hostage
by Theodore Taylor; Delacorte 1988. (4-5)
A Canadian boy is stunned when his efforts to
capture a trapped whale are misinterpreted.

LITERATURE SELECTIONS

❂ Whales
by Rhoda Blumberg; Doubleday 1987. (2-4)
Huge paintings and intriguing facts about whales.

❂ Whales of the World
by June Behrens; Childrens 1987. (2-3)
Explores major species of dolphins and whales, their
habitats and behavior.

❂ A First Look at Whales
by Millicet Selsam; Walker LB 1980. (2-3)
Descriptions of whales that show the various species
and how they differ from fish.

❂ Crystal; The Story of a Real Baby Whale
by Karen C. Smyth; Down East 1986. (3-4)
Follows Crystal, a humpback whale, through her first
year of life.

❂ Whales and Dolphins
by Lionel Bender; Gloucester 1988. (3-4)
Describes how whales and dolphins live, play and
survive in their ocean environment.

❂ Whales, the Nomads of the Sea
by Jean Zallinger; Lothrop 1987. (3-5)
An introduction to whales in text and drawings plus
an extensive glossary.

❂ Humphrey the Wrong-Way Whale
by Kathryn Allen Goldner; Dillon 1987. (4-5)
The story of a whale who swam into San Francisco
Bay and the attempts to help him return to sea.

❂ Rescue of the Stranded Whales
by Kenneth Mallory; Simon & Schuster 1989. (5)
A fascinating story of the rescue operation of whales
stranded amidst ice floes.

RELATED STUDIES & ACTIVITY

● Mammals ● Dolphins ● Porpoises ● Ocean Life ● Migration ●
❂ Work in cooperative groups to make life-sized murals of specific whale species. ❂

List three words found in the story that describe a whale or dolphin.

 What problem did the whale have? How was it solved?
If you read a non-fiction book, tell about a problem whales face.

 If you could talk to the whale in the book, what advice would you give it?

 Retell an interesting part of the story or share a fact you learned about whales (or dolphins).

● Fiction ●
LITERATURE SELECTIONS

● **The Bravest Babysitter**
by Barbara Greenberg; Puffin 1989. (2-3)
When a thunderstorm hits, Lisa becomes her
babysitter's babysitter in this role-reversal story.

● **Time of Wonder**
by Robert McCloskey; Viking 1957. (2-4)
Poetic text describing a summer on the Maine coast
and the hurricane that hits it.

● **Belinda's Hurricane**
by Elizabeth Winthrop; Dutton 1984. (3-4)
Belinda experiences a hurricane on Fox Island with
Granny May, cranky Mr. Fletcher and his bulldog.

● **The Day of the Blizzard**
by Marietta Moskin; Coward 1978. (3-4)
With her mother sick and her father away, Katie goes
on an important errand during a blizzard.

● **Trapped on the Golden Flyer**
by Susan Fleming; Westminster 1978. (4-5)
A boy and 200 passengers spend days on a train
marooned in a blizzard.

● **Anna**
by Mary Stolz; Harper & Row 1988. (4-5)
Grandfather tells the story of how he overcame his
boyhood fear of thunderstorms.

● **Courage at Indian Deep**
by Jane Resh Thomas; Houghton 1984. (5)
A young boy must help save a ship caught in a
sudden storm.

● **Snow Bound**
by Harry Mazer; Dell 1977. (5)
Tony and Cindy spend 11 snowbound days
together in an attempt to survive a fierce storm.

● Non-Fiction ●
LITERATURE SELECTIONS

● **Keep the Lights Burning, Abbie**
by Peter & Connie Coop; Carolrhoda 1985. (2-3)
The story of a girl who keeps the lighthouse lights lit
for four stormy weeks while her father is away.

● **Thunder Cake**
by Patricia Polacco; Philomel 1990. (2-3)
A child overcomes her fear of thunderstorms by
baking a cake with her grandmother before a storm.

● **It's Raining Cats and Dogs**
by Franklyn M. Branley; Houghton 1987. (3-4)
Strange happenings are mixed with scientific
accounts of weather.

● **A Walk in the Snow**
by Phyllis S. Busch; Harper 1971. (2-4)
Photographs show winter scenes and help to answer
questions about snow.

● **Frozen Fire**
by James Houston; McElderry Books 1992. (3-5)
Based on a true ordeal, two boys brave seventy-five
miles in a snow storm to find their father.

● **Storms**
by Ray Broekel; Childrens LB 1982. (3-5)
Reveals the causes and effects of a variety of storms.

● **Blizzards and Winter Weather**
by Dennis B. Fradin; Childrens LB 1983. (4-5)
An account of the causes and effects of blizzards, plus
a history of the most important ones.

● **Disastrous Hurricanes and Tornadoes**
by Max & Charlotte Alth; Watts LB 1981. (4-5)
Learn the origins of these storms and read about some
of the most famous and devastating ones.

RELATED STUDIES & ACTIVITY

● Weather ● Thunder ● Lightning ● Weather Forecasting ● Seasons ● Survival ●
● Prepare and present a weather report for a television newscast. ●

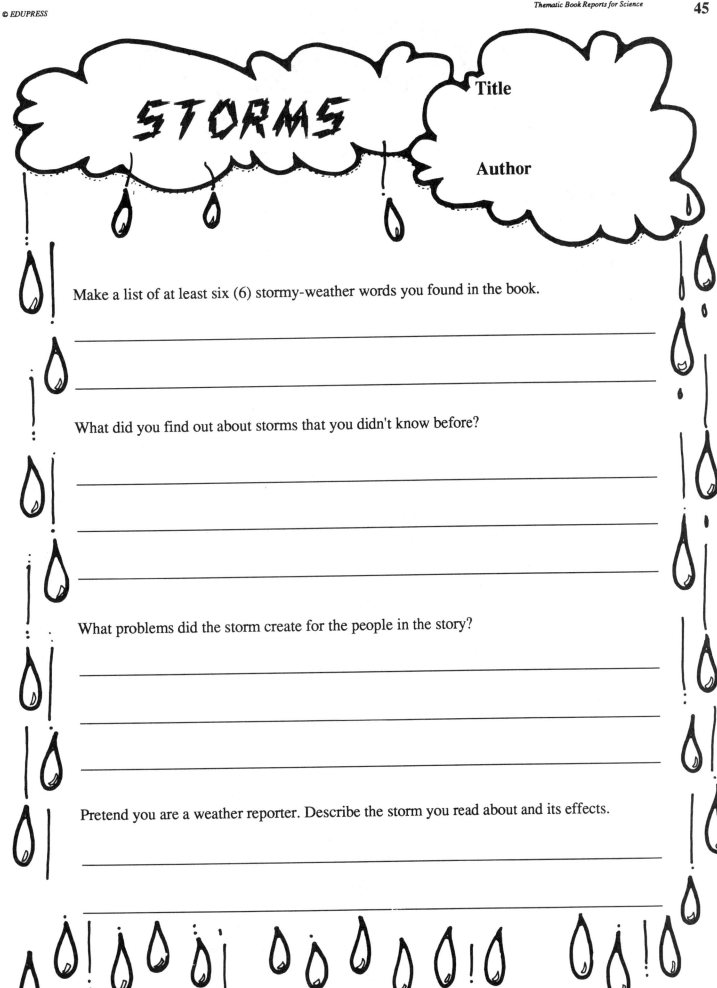

STORMS

Title

Author

Make a list of at least six (6) stormy-weather words you found in the book.

_____

_____

What did you find out about storms that you didn't know before?

_____

_____

_____

What problems did the storm create for the people in the story?

_____

_____

_____

Pretend you are a weather reporter. Describe the storm you read about and its effects.

_____

_____

LITERATURE SELECTIONS

❋ *Robot-Bot-Bot*
by Fernando Krahn; Dutton 1979. (2-3)
A little girl decides to rewire a robot who has been
doing housework.

❋ *Ready, Set, Robot!*
by Lillian and Phoebe Hoban; Harper LB 1982. (2-3)
A robot, Sol-1, competes in a space race.

❋ *My Robot Buddy*
by Alfred Slote; Lippincott 1975. (2-3)
Jack must save his new robot companion, Danny
One, from robot-nappers.

❋ *The Robot Birthday*
by Eve Bunting; Dutton 1980. (3-4)
A robot arrives on the scene and helps ease the
problems of twins Pam and Kerry.

❋ *Norby, The Mixed-up Robot*
by Janet and Isaac Asimov; Walker LB 1984. (3-5)
Jeff, his brother Fargo and a robot named Norby
combat Ing the Ingrate.

❋ *The Type One Super Robot*
by Alison Prince; Macmillan 1988. (4-5)
Young Humbert and his robot, Manders, pay a visit to
Uncle Bellamy.

❋ *C.L.U.T.Z.*
by Marilyn Wilkes; Dial LB 1985. (4-5)
The Pentax family gets a new robot that turns out to
be a clumsy clutz.

❋ *Orvis*
by H. M. Hoover; Puffin 1991. (4-5)
Orvis, an outcast robot in need of a home, runs away
to be with two friends.

LITERATURE SELECTIONS

❋ *Get Ready for Robots!*
by Patricia Lauber; Harper LB 1987. (2-3)
An introduction to robots that work in space, under
water and in factories.

❋ *Robots*
by Carol Greene; Childrens LB 1983. (2-3)
A broad, simple introduction for young readers.

❋ *Robots and Computers*
by Nigel Hawkes; Watts LB 1984. (3-4)
How computers function in robots, plus specialized
robots used in industry, space and the military.

❋ *Robots*
by Hilary Henson; Warwick 1982. (3-4)
Recounts the history of mechanical marvels in fact
and fiction and describes a robot's brain.

❋ *Robotics Basics*
by Karen Liptak; Prentice LB 1984. (3-5)
A fine introduction to the subject that includes a
history of the first programmed robots from 1939.

❋ *Robots*
by Art Kleiner; Raintree LB 1981. (4-5)
Robot mechanisms and their possible uses are
explored.

❋ *Working Robots*
by Fred D'Ignazio; Lodestar 1982. (4-5)
Information on working robots having "senses" and
under computer control and their impact on society.

❋ *Radical Robots*
by George Harrar; Simon & Schuster 1990. (4-5)
Could you be replaced by a robot? Find out what
robots can—and cannot—do.

RELATED STUDIES & ACTIVITY

● Simple Machines ● Inventions ● Science Fiction ● Computers ● Tools ●
● Challenge children to use recycled materials to invent a robot with moving parts. ●

Write a "Things To Do" list for the robot you read about,
based on what you learned it can do.

Things To Do

ROBOTS

Title

Author

Would the robot you read about be a help or a
problem in your life? Explain.

Does the robot you read about have
feelings? How do you know?
Find evidence in the book?

Could a robot *really* have feelings?
Explain your answer.

Fiction

LITERATURE SELECTIONS

The Elephant's Airplane and Other Machines
by Anne-Marie Dalmais; Western 1984. (2)
Raccoon is a fantastic inventor and we see many of
his innovative vehicles.

Mr. Murphy's Marvelous Invention
by Eileen Christelow; Clarion 1983. (2)
A father pig's new housework machine misdoes all
the chores.

Wonder Kid Meets the Evil Lunch Snatcher
by Lois Duncan; Little,Brown 1988. (2-4)
Tormented by bullies, Brian invents Wonder Kid, a
superhero who always triumphs over evil.

Peter Graves
by William Pene du Bois; Puffin 1991. (4-5)
Determined to earn money to rebuild an inventor's
house, Peter puts his mind to work marketing them.

Almost Famous
by David Getz; Henry Holt 1992. (4-5)
Maxine wants to be a famous inventor who thinks she
has found the perfect partner.

Minski
by Arthur Yorinks; Farrar 1988. (4-5)
Young Minski is a brilliant inventor, but longs to be a
singer.

Ben and Me
by Robert Lawson; Little, Brown 1939. (4-5)
Amos, a mouse, takes credit for many of Benjamin
Franklin's inventions and success.

The Blossoms and the Green Phantom
by Betsy Byars; Delacorte 1987. (5)
Junior launches his invention of a hot-air balloon and
hopes everyone will mistake it for a flying saucer.

Non-Fiction

LITERATURE SELECTIONS

Gutenberg
by Leonard Everett Fisher; Macmillan 1992. (2-4)
Gutenberg had a vision. He wanted to invent a
mechanical method of printing and producing copies.

**Shoes for Everyone: A Story about Jan
Matzeliger**
by Barbara Mitchell; Carolrhoda 1986. (3-5)
The life of the black inventor and his inventions.

The Best of Rube Goldberg
by Rube Goldberg; Prentice Hall 1979. (3-5)
Ingenious and elaborate mechanical inventions of
outlandish necessities.

Weird and Wacky Inventions
by Jim Murphy; Crown 1978. (3-5)
Ninety of the oddest inventions patented by the U.S.
Patent Trademark office.

**Why Didn't I Think of That? From Alarm Clocks
to Zippers**
by Webb Garrison; Prentice Hall 1977. (4-5)
Over sixty stories behind ingenious inventions.

What's the Big Idea, Ben Franklin?
by Jean Fritz; Coward 1976. (4-5)
An entertaining and astonishing account that reveals
details and marvels of Benjamin Franklin.

Guess Again: More Weird & Wacky Inventions
by Jim Murphy; Bradbury 1986. (3-5)
Examples of some of the off-the-wall devices that
have already been patented.

Nature Invented It First
by Ross E. Hutchins; Dodd 1980. (4-5)
An explanation of how many inventions such as sonar
first occurred in nature.

RELATED STUDIES & ACTIVITY

● Inventors ● Machines ● Technology ● Biographies ●

● Choose a simple invention to share. Explain how it has made life different. ●

Describe an invention in the book. What made it special or different?

_____

_____

_____

Write a few sentences telling about the inventor of this invention. _____

_____

_____

_____

How did the invention change the lives of the people in the story or the people who used it? _____

_____

_____

Do you think the invention was useful? Tell why or why not. _____

_____

Inventions

Title

Author

_____   _____

OUTER SPACE

● Fiction ●

LITERATURE SELECTIONS

❋ **Space Case**
by Edward Marshall; Dial 1980. (2)
Buddy befriends a space creature who repays the
favor by posing as his school space project.

❋ **Alistair in Outer Space**
by Marilyn Sadler; Prentice 1984. (2)
Nerdy Alistair is carried off by a spaceship on his
way to the library.

❋ **We're Back**
by Hudson Talbott; Crown 1987. (2-3)
Seven dinosaurs are taken from their primitive planet
onto a spaceship by alien Vorb.

❋ **The Spaceship Under the Apple Tree**
by Louis Slobodkin; Collier 1952. (3-4)
Earth boy, Eddie, befriends and helps cover up for
Marty, a science explorer from the planet Martinea.

❋ **The Space Ship Returns to the Apple Tree**
by Louis Slobodkin; Macmillan 1972. (3-5)
Eddie and his friend from a distant planet share
adventures.

❋ **The Fallen Spaceman**
by Lee Harding; Bantam 1982. (3-4)
Two boys discover the enormous spacesuit that holds
Tyro, an alien trapped on Earth.

❋ **Stinker From Space**
by Pamela Service; Scribner 1988. (3-5)
Tsynq Yr takes on a new life form—that of a skunk—
in his desperate attempt to escape an enemy on Earth.

❋ **Calling B for Butterfly**
by Louise Lawrence; Harper LB 1982. (5)
Four teenagers and two children are the only
survivors of a starliner smashed by an asteroid.

● Non-Fiction ●

LITERATURE SELECTIONS

❋ **Is There Life in Outer Space?**
by Franklin M. Branley; Harper LB 1984. (2-3)
In cartoon format, the intriguing question of life in
outer space is explored for the young.

❋ **Journey Into a Black Hole**
by Franklin M. Branley; Harper LB 1986. (2-3)
A young traveler in space journeys into a black hole
in this scientific explanation.

❋ **On The Moon**
by Jenny Vaughan; Watts LB 1983. (2-3)
Join the astronauts on a flight into space and relive the
first moon landing.

❋ **Space Walking**
by Gregory Vogt; Watts LB 1987. (3-4)
Step into a space suit and find out about space
walkers and future space walks.

❋ **To Space and Back**
by Sally Ride; Lothrop 1986. (3-5)
The first American woman in space describes her
experiences aboard the shuttle.

❋ **The Story of the Challenger Disaster**
by Zachary Kent; Childrens 1986. (3-5)
An account of the disaster that befell the space shuttle
Challenger.

❋ **Nova: Space Explorer's Guide**
by Richard Maurer; Random House 1991. (4-5)
Experience the simulation of an actual space voyage
and space exploration.

❋ **See Inside a Space Station**
by Robin Kerrod; Watts 1988. (4-5)
Find out about the activities and experiments inside a
future station in space.

RELATED STUDIES & ACTIVITY

● Astronauts ● Planets ● UFOs ● Distance ● Explorers ● Gravity ● Speed ● Rockets ●
● Use large boxes and recycled materials to construct a spaceship for role-playing. ●

Title

Author

Complete this "eyewitness" story for the *Space Daily News.*

Imagine that you were with the people or characters in the book you read and report on your adventures.

SPACE DAILY NEWS

A Newspaper of Space Activity and Exploration

My experience involving outer space began when

My space companion was

You would have been amazed to see

The most dangerous part was when

Things would have ended differently if

In the future, I think

• Fiction •

LITERATURE SELECTIONS

❋ *The Great Green Turkey Creek Monster*
by James Flora; Atheneum 1976. (2-3)
Growing madly by the minute, the almost
unstoppable Great Green Hooligan Vine escapes.

❋ *The Night the Monster Came*
by Mary Calhoun; Morrow 1982. (2-3)
Andy fears Big Foot is responsible for the huge
animal-like footprints in the snow.

❋ *A Special Trick*
by Mercer Mayer; Dial 1976. (2-3)
Ellroy tries out a magician's monster-filled book of
magic spells and calls up a six-eyed galaplops.

❋ *Dorrie and the Dreamyard Monsters*
by Patricia Coombs; Dell 1977. (2-4)
Dorrie helps convert fierce monsters into lovable
friends in this adventure story.

❋ *The Iron Giant: A Story in Five Nights*
by Ted Hughes; Harper & Row 1988. (3-4)
The metal-devouring giant settles in a junkyard until
a space-bat-angel-dragon threatens Earth.

❋ *My Friend the Monster*
by Clyde Robert Bulla; Harper LB 1980. (3-5)
Prince Hal tries to gain access to a mountain where he
believes monsters live.

❋ *Kneeknock Rise*
by Natalie Babbitt; Sunburst 1970. (4-5)
Villagers think that a fearsome creature they call
Megrimum lives at the top of Kneeknock Rise.

❋ *The Monster Garden*
by Vivien Alcock; Delacorte 1988. (5)
Frankie incubates a bit of living tissue in a petri dish
and raises a fast-growing, nonhuman creature.

• Non-Fiction •

LITERATURE SELECTIONS

❋ *Living Monsters: The World's Most Dangerous
Animals*
by Howard Tomb; Schuster 1992. (2-3)
Profiles of 18 deadly animals: sea wasps, army ants.

❋ *The Naked Bear; Folktales of the Iroquois*
by John Bierhorst; Morrow 1987. (2-4)
Sixteen traditional Iroquois tales feature talking
animals and horrific monsters.

❋ *Mystery Monsters of Loch Ness*
by Patricia Lauber; Garrard LB 1978. (3-4)
Does this creature really exist? Read this author's
account and judge for yourself.

❋ *Bigfoot and Other Legendary Creatures*
by Paul Robert Walker; Harcourt 1992. (3-5)
Read about the legends of Bigfoot, the monster of
Loch Ness and the modern-day dinosaur of Africa.

❋ *Movie Monsters*
by Thomas Aylesworth; Harper 1975. (4-5)
Background information on the creation of the
"greatest" movie monsters.

❋ *Mad Scientists, Weird Doctors, and Time
Travelers in Movies, TV, and Books*
by Seymour Simon; Harper LB 1981. (4-5)
An introduction to monsters in the mass media.

❋ *On the Track of Bigfoot*
by Marian T. Place; Pocket 1980. (5)
A detailed account of the search for the monster,
Bigfoot, otherwise known as Sasquatch.

❋ *Fabulous Beasts*
by Alison Lurie; Farrar 1981. (5)
Tales of mythical animals immortalized in legends.

RELATED STUDIES & ACTIVITY

• Legends • Animal Tracks • Giants • Fairy Tales • Fact vs. Fiction •
• Invent a monster. Create a mask to match a written description. •

MONSTERS

Title: _____

Author: _____

If you were hunting for the monster you read about,
where would you look?

Retell a part of the story you thought was exciting.

Choose one of these words and explain why it reminds you of the monster you read about:
funny, fierce, lovable, shy, crazy, stubborn, unhappy, dangerous, frightening

Turn the paper over and draw a picture of a monster in the book.
Find words that describe it and write them under the picture.

LITERATURE SELECTIONS

❀ **Too Many Balloons**
by Catherine Malthias; Childrens 1982. (2-3)
Buying one balloon for each animal she sees at the
zoo, a girl eventually has 55 and starts to float away.

❀ **The Big Balloon Race**
by Eleanor Coerr; Harper LB 1981. (2-3)
Arill and her mother fly their balloon in a suspenseful
race.

❀ **That's Good! That's Bad!**
by Margery Cuyler; Henry Holt 1992. (2-3)
A boy's parents give him a balloon that lifts and
carries him on a jungle adventure.

❀ **The Red Balloon**
by Albert Lamorisse; Doubleday 1956. (2-3)
Pascal possesses a magic balloon that leads him on a
tour of Paris.

❀ **Hot-Air Henry**
by Mary Calhoun; Morrow LB 1981. (2-4)
Siamese cat, Henry, sneaks into the basket of a hot air
balloon and soon is afloat.

❀ **Balloon Ride**
by Evelyn Mott; Walker 1991. (3-5)
Megan goes for a ride in a hot-air balloon and learns
all the details of how one is operated.

❀ **Twenty-One Balloons**
by William Pene du Bois; Viking 1947. (4-5)
Truth and fiction are combined in the adventures of a
professor who sails around the world in a balloon.

❀ **The Blossoms and the Green Phantom**
by Betsy Byars; Delacorte 1987. (5)
Junior launches his invention of a hot-air balloon and
hopes everyone will mistake it for a flying saucer.

LITERATURE SELECTIONS

❀ **A Rainbow Balloon: A Book of Concepts**
by Ann Lenssen; Cobblehill Books 1992. (2)
Introduces basic concepts, such as rise and fall, while
following the flight of a hot-air balloon.

❀ **My Balloon**
by Kay Davies; Doubleday 1990. (2-3)
Uses simple activities with a balloon to introduce
basic science concepts.

❀ **Balloon Trip**
by Huck Scarry; Prentice Hall 1983. (3-4)
A bird's-eye view of the world while airborne on
moving currents in a hot-air balloon.

❀ **Balloons, Zeppelins, and Dirigibles**
by Aaron Percefull; Watts 1983. (3-5)
Traces the history of airships from the 18th century to
the present describing inventors, models and blimps.

❀ **Research Balloons: Exploring Hidden Worlds**
by Carole Briggs; Lerner Publications 1998. (4-5)
Describes different kinds of research balloons and the
amazing work they do in expanding our knowledge.

❀ **Balloon Voyage**
by Rupert Saunders; Rourke Enterprises 1988. (4-5)
Describes the trip of the first persons ever to cross the
Atlantic by hot-air balloon.

❀ **Ballooning**
by Carole Briggs; Lerner Publications 1986. (4-5)
Explains how hot air and gas balloons work. Also
describes races, rallies and a typical ride in a balloon.

❀ **Balloons**
by Bernie Zubrowski; Morrow Junior Bks 1990. (5)
Learn about scientific principles that can be
demonstrated with balloons and other inflatable toys.

RELATED STUDIES & ACTIVITY

● Air ● Wind ● Air Currents ● Hot-air Balloons ● Blimps ●

● Conduct balloon experiments. Compare the results of helium-filled and air-filled balloons. ●

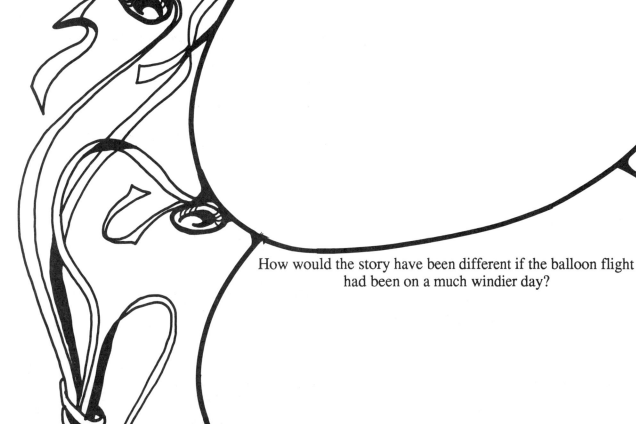

Title

Author

BALLOONS

What kind of balloon did you read about …
… a party balloon? a hot-air balloon?

Turn the paper over and write a description of it.
Ask a classmate to draw a picture
of the balloon based on
the description.

Find and write an example from
the story that shows how air
affected the balloon.

Take a ride in the balloon
you read about. Describe what you saw
on your trip.

How would the story have been different if the balloon flight
had been on a much windier day?

● Fiction ●

LITERATURE SELECTIONS

❋ *Nothing to Do*
by Peter Spier; Doubleday 1978. (2)
Two enterprising brothers scour the house for parts
for an airplane they decide to build.

❋ *Alistair's Time Machine*
by Marilyn Sadler; Prentice Hall 1986. (2)
Scientist Alistair's new time machine takes him to a
French palace, pirate ship and prehistoric campsite.

❋ *The Brain on Quartz Mountain*
by Margaret Anderson; Knopf 1982. (3-4)
David helps an eccentric professor educate a growing
chicken brain.

❋ *Mr. Twigg's Mistake*
by Robert Lawson; Little 1985. (3-5)
A pet mole gets an overdose of vitamin X, a growth
vitamin, with unexpected results.

❋ *Eaton Stanley and the Mind Control Experiment*
by David Adler; Dutton 1985. (4-5)
Precocious Eaton decides to take control of his sixth-
grade teacher's mind for his science project.

❋ *Top Secret*
by John Reynolds Gardiner; Little 1985. (5)
Allen pursues his science project of human
photosynthesis until he turns into a green plant.

❋ *Project: Genius*
by William Hayes; Atheneum 1962. (5)
Pete attempts to win first prize for his school's most
original outside project, when it backfires.

❋ *Nutty Knows All*
by Dean Hughes; Atheneum 1988. (5)
Nutty Nutsell goes to the science fair with an
experiment of protons that make his head glow.

● Non-Fiction ●

LITERATURE SELECTIONS

❋ *The Sun, the Wind and the Rain*
by Lisa Westberg Peters; Henry Holt 1988. (2)
Elizabeth constructs a sand "mountain" at the beach,
only to have it erode from wind and rain.

❋ *The Quicksand Book*
by Tomie de Paola; Holiday House 1977. (2-3)
Jungle Boy lectures Jungle Girl on the facts behind
quicksand and how not to sink in it.

❋ *Shark Lady: True Adventures of Eugenie Clark*
by Ann McGovern; Macmillan 1979. (3-4)
An account of the work and accomplishments of this
scientist and director of a marine laboratory.

❋ *The Story of Nim, the Chimp Who Learned
   Language*
by Anna Michel; Knopf 1980. (3-5)
Nim, a chimpanzee, learns American sign language.

❋ *William Beebe: Underwater Explorer*
by Wyatt Blassingame; Garrard LB 1976. (3-4)
Find out about the scientist's underwater exploits and
experiments.

❋ *The Wright Brothers at Kitty Hawk*
by Donald J. Sobol; Scholastic 1987. (4-5)
The exciting story of two brothers and their scientific
experiments with flight.

❋ *Science in Egypt*
by Geraldine Woods; Watts 1988. (5)
Find out about discoveries of this ancient civilization,
such as the mummification process.

❋ *Secret in a Sealed Bottle: Lazzaro Spallanzani's
   Work with Microbes*
by Sam and Beryl Epstein; Coward 1979. (5)
Lazzaro's brilliant experiments with animacules.

RELATED STUDIES & ACTIVITY

● Scientists ● Research ● Scientific Method ● Inventions ●
● Conduct science experiments in cooperative groups. Share the results. ●

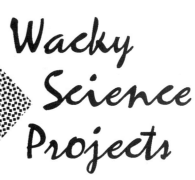

Wacky Science Projects

Title

Author

Write a **Scientific Report**
based on the plot and information
you read in the book.

Scientist —— What information can you share about the scientist in the story?

Materials —— What was used to in order to conduct this experiment?

Methods —— Step-by-step, what did the scientist do in the experiment?

Observations —— What happened? What were the results of the experiment?

Conclusions —— What was learned that can be shared with the scientific world?

● Fiction ●

LITERATURE SELECTIONS

● *Gregory, the Terrible Eater*
by Mitchell Sharmat; Four Winds 1984. (2)
Concerned goat parents worry when their son refuses
to eat junk.

● *Cranberry Thanksgiving*
by Harry & Wendy Devlin; Macmillan 1980. (2)
Grandmother suspects the wrong man of stealing her
famous cranberry bread recipe.

● *Beats Me, Claude*
by Joan Lowery Nixon; Viking 1986. (2-3)
Each time Shirley bakes an apple pie, she leaves out a
vital ingredient which causes mayhem with a robber.

● *How to Eat Fried Worms*
by Thomas Rockwell; Franklin Watts 1973. (3-4)
A bet to eat a worm a day for 15 days for $50 is
accepted by Billy, who claims he can eat anything.

● *Fat Men From Space*
by Daniel Pinkwater; Dodd, Mead 1977. (3-4)
Aliens plan to invade Earth, rob it of its junk food and
make Earthlings their slaves.

● *Stone Soup*
by Marcia Brown; Scribner 1947. (2-4)
In a French village, some hungry soldiers teach the
stingy villagers a cooking lesson.

● *Iduna and the Magic Apples*
by Marianna Mayer; Macmillan 1988. (4-5)
A beloved mistress grows apples that keep Odin and
the other gods forever young.

● *The Search for Delicious*
by Natalie Babbitt; Farrar 1985. (4-5)
The kingdom is in violent disagreement over which
food best fits the new definition of "delicious."

● Non-Fiction ●

LITERATURE SELECTIONS

● *Let's Eat!*
by True Kelley; Dutton 1986. (2)
An appetizing look at where food comes from and
how people eat it.

● *The Popcorn Book*
by Tomie dePaola; Holiday LB 1987. (2-3
While Tony makes a plate of popcorn, Tiny tells
interesting facts about this delicious food.

● *Nutrition*
by Leslie Jean LeMaster; Childrens 1985. (2-3)
Facts on nutrition are highlighted with color photos
for beginning readers.

● *All About Bread*
by Geoffrey Patterson; Dutton 1985. (2-4)
Learn about bread-milling techniques, bread baking
and modern bakeries.

● *Ice Cream*
by William Jaspersohn; Macmillan 1988. (3-5)
Find out how ice cream is made by touring Ben and
Jerry's ice cream plant in Vermont.

● *Junk Food—What It Is, What It Does*
by Judith S. Seixas; Greenwillow LB 1984. (2-5)
An account of food that contains many calories but
not much nutrition.

● *A Book of Vegetables*
by Harriet Langsam Sobol; Putnam 1984. (3-5)
Learn how fourteen different vegetables are grown.

● *Rice*
by Sylvia A. Johnson; Lerner 1985. (4-5)
Clear photos and text explain the process of growing
this food.

RELATED STUDIES & ACTIVITY

● Diet ● Health ● Food Groups ● Nutrition ● Vitamins ●

● Make a collage with magazine pictures to represent one of the basic food groups ●

FOOD

Title _____   **Author** _____

Write a short summary of the story or book content.

Pretend you are a chef.
Plan a meal that includes the food you read about in the book. Make it balanced!

Make a list of words that describe the food in the story.

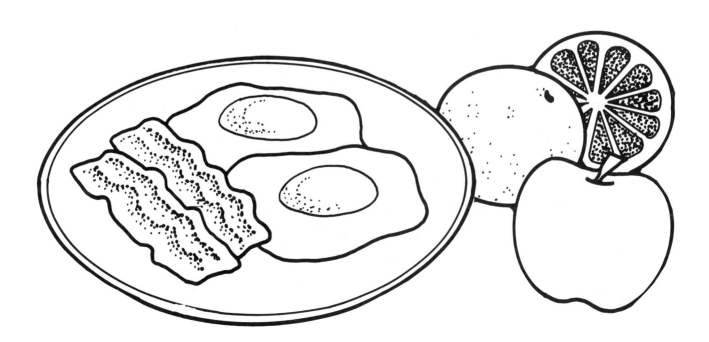

SENSES

● Fiction ●

LITERATURE SELECTIONS

❋ *Through Grandpa's Eyes*
by Patricia MacLachlan; HarperCollins 1980. (2-3)
John learns to appreciate that ,even though his
grandpa is blind, he moves through a detailed world.

❋ *The Conversation Club*
by Diane Stanley; Aladdin 1990. (2-3)
A mouse, who loves to listen, starts a club where his
friends learn there's more to conversation than talk.

❋ *The Other Way to Listen*
by Byrd Baylor; Macmillan 1978. (2-3)
An old man teaches a young boy how to listen.

❋ *The Search For Delicious*
by Natalie Babbitt; Sunburst 1991. (4-5)
There is a disagreement over the definition of the
word "delicious" for the new royal dictionary.

❋ *The Chocolate Touch*
by Patrick Catling; Bantam 1979. (4-5)
Everything that John touches turns—not to gold—but
a rich, dark chocolate.

❋ *Blind Outlaw*
by Glen Rounds; Holiday 1980. (4-5)
A mute boy lassoes a blind horse.

❋ *The Sweet Touch*
by Lorna Balian; Abingdon 1976. (4-5)
Tiny Genie's spell causes everything Peggy touches
to turn into candy.

❋ *Follow My Leader*
by James B. Garfield; Viking 1957. (4-5)
After being blinded by a firecracker, 11-year-old
Jimmy slowly adjusts to his handicap.

● Non-Fiction ●

LITERATURE SELECTIONS

❋ *Claire and Emma*
by Diana Peter; Harper LB 1977. (2-4)
Two sisters, though deaf, fit into the family's
activities.

❋ *Anna's Silent World*
by Bernard Wolf; Harper 1977. (2-4)
The story of a deaf girl who attends classes with
children who have normal hearing.

❋ *Mom's Best Friend*
by Sally Hobart Alexander; Macmillan 1992. (2-4)
Ursula, a seeing-eye dog, is sent to help a blind
mother keep a house running smoothly.

❋ *Amy: The Story of a Deaf Child*
by Lou Ann Walker; Lodestar 1985. (2-4)
A photo essay describing the everyday activities of
fifth-grader, Amy Bowley, who is deaf.

❋ *Burnish Me Bright*
by Julia Cunningham; Peter Smith 1980. (3-5)
Based on fact, an imaginative mute boy is scorned by
the inhabitants of the French village where he lives.

❋ *Child of the Silent Night: The Story of Laura Bridgman*
by Edith Fisher Hunter; Houghton 1963. (3-5)
The first blind, deaf, and mute person to be
successfully taught to communicate.

❋ *Our Mom*
by Kay Burns; Watts LB 1989. (3-5)
A paraplegic mother struggles to raise four children.

❋ *Helen Keller: Toward the Light*
by Stewart Graff/Polly Graff; Garrad LB 1964. (3-5)
A biography of the woman who overcame the
handicaps of blindness and deafness.

RELATED STUDIES & ACTIVITY

● Disabilities ● Temperature ● Television ● Radio ● Animal Sounds ●
● Form five cooperative groups to create displays——one for each sense. ●

Title

Author

SENSES

Circle the sense (or senses) the story was mainly about:

Touch • Sight • Smell • Hearing • Taste

How did this "sense" affect the life of the main character in the story?

If you could improve one of the five senses for the main character, which one would it be and why?

If you could ask the main character a question about one of the five senses, what would it be?

SKELETONS

● Fiction ●

LITERATURE SELECTIONS

● *Funnybones*
by Janet and Allen Ahlberg; Greenwillow 1980. (2)
A big and a little skeleton take their dog skeleton for a walk through town and look for someone to scare.

● *The Amazing Bone*
by William Steig; Farrar 1976. (2-3)
Pearl the Pig's loyal talking bone saves her from a hungry fox.

● *Hob Goblin and the Skeleton*
by Alice Schertle; Lothrop LB 1982. (2-3)
Hob Goblin needs a new helper, but Halloween night is not the time to find one.

● *Big Old Bones: A Dinosaur Tale*
by Carol Carrick; Ticknor 1989. (2-3)
Professor Potts finds a bunch of old bones to take back East to assemble.

● *The Curse of the Egyptian Mummy*
by Pat Hutchins; Greenwillow 1983. (3-5)
Legend surrounding the mummified body of an ancient Egyptian pharoah.

● *Jeremy Visick*
by David Wiseman; Houghton Mifflin 1981. (5)
Matthew is driven to find the remains of a 12-year-old boy lost in a mining accident in his town.

● *The Tar Pit*
by Tor Seidler; Farrar 1987. (5)
Edward retreats to an old tar pit and discovers a dinosaur jawbone.

● *Tales Mummies Tell*
by Patricia Lauber; Crowell 1985. (5)
Tales of what scientists have discovered about ancient life from well-preserved human remains.

● Non-Fiction ●

LITERATURE SELECTIONS

● *What Am I Made Of?*
by David Bennett; Aladdin 1992. (2)
Learn the fascinating facts about the skeleton hidden inside your skin.

● *A First Look at Animals with Backbones*
by Millicent Selsam; Walker LB 1978. (2-3)
An introduction to scientific classification and vertebrates.

● *Supersaurus*
by Francine Jacobs; Putnam LB 1982. (2-3)
The true story of the discovery of bones from a giant dinosaur.

● *Prehistoric People*
by Ovid K. Wong; Childrens 1988. (2-4)
Find out how scientists use human remains to gather information.

● *Digging Up Dinosaurs*
by Aliki; Crowell 1981. (2-4)
A behind-the-scenes look at what's involved in digging up and reconstructing dinosaur skeletons.

● *Whales*
by Joan Bonnett Wexo; Wildlife 1983. (3-4)
Contains fascinating views of a whale's skeletal structure.

● *Talking Bones: Secrets of Indian Mound Builders*
by William O. Steele; Harper LB 1978. (4-5)
Findings from studies on prehistoric burial grounds.

● *Shells Are Skeletons*
by Joan Berg Victor; Crowell 1977. (2-4)
A fascinating report on sea animals belonging to the mollusk family.

RELATED STUDIES & ACTIVITY

● Vertebrates ● Dinosaurs ● Archaeology ● Fossils ● Human Body ● Mollusks & Shells ●
● Examine a variety of clean, dry bones through a magnifying glass. ●

Title

SKELETONS

Author

> You are an archaeologist, 300 years from now. You have just discovered the bones or skeleton you read about in the story.
>
> It is your job to report to your fellow scientists, what you learned from the bones and skeletons you discovered.
>
> Write your report below.

The Discovery:

What:

Where:

How:

What We Can Learn

Size:

When it lived:

What life may have been like then:

More Exciting Titles from **Edupress**

102 **Indian Activity Book**
Art•Crafts•Cooking

126 **Colonial Activities**
Art•Crafts•Cooking

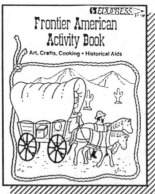

138 **Frontier Activities**
Art•Crafts•Cooking

128 **Easy Book Projects**
Report, explore, share

134 **Holiday Games**
Fun-filled learning

135 **Center Games**
Ten easy game centers

136 **Outdoor Games**
Group and skill games

137 **Desktop Games**
Indoor learning games

140 **Classroom Kickoff**
Year-long resource

139 **Super Arts & Crafts**
Over 700 art activities

134 **Oodles of Writing**
Hundreds of prompts

150 **Books, Bulletin Boards**
Publish & display

130 **Fall Projects**
Multicurricular learning

131 **Winter Projects**
Loads of winter activities

132 **Spring Projects**
Apr/May/June fun

148 **Springboards & Starters**
Over 1000 learning sparks